Reading, Writing and Relevance
Mary Hoffman

Hodder and Stoughton
In association with the United Kingdom Reading Association

ISBN 0 340 21025 7

Printed and bound in Great Britain for
Hodder and Stoughton Educational,
a division of Hodder and Stoughton Limited, London,
by Cox & Wyman Ltd, London, Fakenham and Reading

Contents

Acknowledgments

The author and publishers would like to thank the following for permission to use material in this book:
Longman Group Ltd, for material which originally appeared in *Educating the Consumer*, by Alma Williams (1975); pp. 39 and 42, pp. 54–9, pp. 60–3, p. 159, pp. 177–8, and pp. 178–81; *The Times Educational Supplement* (Scotland) for material originally printed in *Planning their own New Town*, by Margaret Ross (22.3.1974); Forbes Publications Ltd, for material originally contained in the article *Souvenir Seventy-Four* by Alma Williams, in *Consumer Education*, September 1974.

In addition the author would like to thank the following people for contributing examples and suggestions:
Miss Dorothy Latham, Headmistress of Dymchurch Primary School, Kent, her children and staff; Michael Gale and his students on a one-year course in reading at Digby Stuart College of Education, Roehampton, London; Donald Moyle and his students on a one-year course in reading at Edge Hill College of Education, Ormskirk; Margaret Peters and her students on a one-year course in reading at the Institute of Education in Cambridge; Alma Williams, Education Consultant to the Consumer Association and consultant to the Open University's Reading Development course; Mary Vambe of the Richard Clondesley School for Physically Handicapped Children, London; The Schools Curriculum Project, Queen's University, Belfast; pupils and staff of St Rose's Secondary School, Belfast; pupils and staff of Hampstead School, London; Janet Maybin and Keith Livingstone of The Open University's Post-Experience Unit; Vicky Austerfield, a remedial teacher at an ILEA school; Margaret Milne and her pupils at Stonehouse Primary School, Lanarkshire; and lastly, but for obvious reasons not least, the staff, pupils and guinea-pigs of Hursthead County Infants School, Cheadle Hulme, Cheshire.

The two photographs on pages 29 and 42 are reproduced by permission of the Open University, from course PE261, *Reading Development*. All other photographs were taken by Brian Long.

Preface

So many books are being published in the educational field today that it is very difficult for teachers to keep in touch with new developments. This series of monographs has been devised both to collate new ideas and to save teachers of reading from having to spend so much of their valuable time searching out relevant texts and materials.

Each monograph deals with a specific aspect of reading. This monograph is a collection of reports of classroom activities. In presenting these, the author concentrates on the context within which reading can be encouraged, rather than on the minutiae of how to teach specific skills. There is a major emphasis on purposes for reading—the child's own purposes as well as the teachers' purposes.

The author is a journalist and a children's writer, an English graduate who is also qualified in linguistics. She is able, therefore, to present a lively account of the various activities which she reports and to capture their essential flavour in terms of the experiences of the children involved. At the same time, she is able to highlight those aspects which offer the best kinds of opportunity for developing language skills in general and reading in particular.

This monograph is not intended to provide a recipe for all to follow, although it does provide some useful additions for the repertoire. Primarily, however, it is intended as a stimulus—and to provide moral support for those teachers who believe that children must be taught how to make their own decisions and follow them through. Independent reading is part of that process.

Professor J. E. Merritt
Faculty of Educational Studies
The Open University, Milton Keynes

I

Introduction

1.1   It all began with a guinea-pig in Cheadle Hulme. Ronald Johnson, Senior Inspector for Primary Education in Cheshire, had been school-spotting for television programmes to accompany the Open University's course in Reading Development, for which he was a consultant. When he saw the children of Hursthead County Infants' School using a hand-made book of instructions to help them look after their classroom pet, he knew he had found a good way of demonstrating functional reading. Months later, when I was talking to Professor John Merritt, the Advisory Editor to this series, about the possibility of a monograph on relevant reading activities, he was still thinking about that guinea-pig. As Chairman of the Reading Development course, Professor Merritt was both delighted with this particular example of children reading to further their own goals and disturbed to find that so few others had come to light as the broadcasts were being made. In the course of many discussions, what we understood to be a real 'guinea-pig activity', as it came to be known, became more clearly defined. It seems worth setting down at the start what underlies these notions of reading, writing and relevance.

1.2   *Relevance to whom?* The activity should have relevance to the children who are actually involved in reading or writing. They need to be able to see *why* these extraordinary activities are necessary or worthwhile, not just to be told that they are. 'Teacher would get cross when you get older if you couldn't read,' said one infant who was asked why people read, and pleasing teacher is very often the only motive children have to sustain them through the acquisition of this complex set of skills. Some children do see the point of reading straight away, as other replies to the question show—'So you can read where the buses are going,' and 'When you go swimming you know how deep it is'—but for many the reasons for reading remain a mystery. So a guinea-pig activity involves children in reading or writing which develops naturally out of needs and goals of their own.

Who decides? At one stage I wondered if, to be really relevant to children's own life experience, reading and writing should always be the result of their spontaneous suggestions. But this appeared early on to be a counsel of perfection; teacher-contrivance or initiation seems to be no hindrance to genuine interest and involvement for the children. What does seem crucial is for the children themselves to be involved at every stage. This includes deciding what to do and why, as well as planning activities. It is vital for children not to have these important stages taken over and done for them by their teacher. Whether what is being planned is a rota for 'wombling' in the infant playground or an elaborate questionnaire on local leisure amenities, the principle is the same. The relevance of the reading and writing will first be put to the test at the planning stage and, if the pupils don't recognise it, one important part of their plans may be not to carry those activities out.

How can they tell what is relevant? There must be some reward inherent in the reading and writing that is undertaken which, if not immediate, is not so far deferred that the children themselves cannot anticipate it. To take a clear example, in following a recipe for baking cakes, reading is strongly motivated by the desire to make something edible which is then eaten! But, in one of the cookery examples I have included (11.3), the children were baking a cake for a special occasion and did not eat it for some days. The time-lapse was still short enough for that anticipation, together with excitement about the occasion, to motivate their reading. As children grow older, the time that elapses between reading or writing and reward can be longer. By adulthood, for some people, that gap may be years. But for a young child beginning to read, who needs to find out why he is doing it, the gap should be as short as possible.

What is 'relevant' vocabulary? To be relevant, the vocabulary must be familiar to the child and *interesting enough to be worth remembering and using again.* The vocabulary load does not have to be high; with very young children it should be low, but one only has to listen to primary school children talking about dinosaurs to realise that the most memorable words are not necessarily the easiest to say or spell.

The actual spoken vocabulary of young children demonstrates a far greater range and more richness of association than is considered appropriate in reading materials published for their age group. (See S. G. Zimet (1976) *Print and Prejudice*, London: Hodder & Stoughton, Chapter 6, 'Vocabulary Differences'.) This vocabulary can be used most effectively to achieve relevance in the language-experience approach to the teaching of reading. In this approach, children read and write words that are already familiar to them in their speech. In a 'guinea-pig activity' the words used are relevant to some goal decided on by the children themselves and so inevitably are of the greatest personal relevance and interest.

1.3   These were the main touchstones I used in going out to search for relevant reading and writing activities in schools. The result is this collection of examples, some of which are genuine 'guinea-pig' material, while others need some modification to meet the above criteria. For the practising teachers who read this monograph, it will be clear that it is not an attempt to provide models for copying in their own classroom. What is relevant for one group or individual may say nothing to another and there are few universals in this field. What I have tried to do is gather together examples which will provoke thought, and probably argument too, about what constitutes relevant reading and writing. For this reason, most of the examples are followed by a few leading questions to stimulate evaluation of them. As far as possible, I have used the language of the teachers who described the activities to me and, where children's own materials are quoted, the only editing they have been subjected to is selection.

Mary Hoffman
1976

Part 1

First and Infant School

2
Guinea-pigs and Other Animals

2.1   Pets in the infant classroom provide a useful stimulus for functional writing and reading activities. They need to be fed, watered, cleaned and perhaps groomed. These tasks are often performed by different children each day or each week and organised on the basis of a rota. No individual task is too difficult for a small child to cope with, but remembering all the things that have to be done and what order they have to be done in is not so easy.

2.2   A class of six-year-olds in Kent found that when the instructions for looking after their two guinea-pigs were passed on from one child to the next on the rota, some information would be left out or be reported inaccurately. They made a book of guinea-pig care, pooling all the information that the various children in the class could think of. There had to be a lot of discussion and planning before they could be sure that nothing important had been left out.

2.3   The result was an important manual of information, containing instructions for cleaning out the guinea-pigs' hutch, providing clean and appropriate food and fresh water, and ensuring that the pets can't escape during the process. The instructions were written by some of the children, with help from the teacher where necessary, and often from the dictation of other children in the class. Now when the next child on the rota has to look after the guinea-pigs, he or she reads the manual with a purpose and the animals are well cared for.

2.4   In the same school there are two budgies, Oscar and Billy, who used to live in the classroom. One day, the teacher put the cage out in the corridor and asked the children to write a label explaining what the budgies ate and drank and why they had been banished, so that the other children in the school would know why the birds were there and not feed them unsuitable goodies. One little girl put it quite succinctly:

★ Billy and Oscar eat seeds They are in the corridoor Because they are noisy when we tell stories and they are really noisey all the time They drink water and they have a cuttle bone to bite it and birds are nice.

2.5   Most classroom pets, like hamsters, gerbils, guinea-pigs, mice, rabbits and budgies, will be familiar to some child in the class, who may keep them at home. In the case of a more exotic creature, like a lizard or terrapin, if no one (including the teacher) knows where to start, there is a good opportunity for looking the information up and writing it out. Booklets about most kinds of pet can be obtained from the RSPCA or other agencies.

2.6   A five-year-old girl in a London school brought into class a slow-worm, which her father had found on a building-site. It looked like a snake, and the class-teacher put it in an empty glass goldfish tank, with a lid. The teacher did not draw particular attention to the slow-worm but, after a while, a boy of five came and asked her what they were going to do about feeding it. 'Oh, I think I'll give it a biscuit at break,' she replied and the child went away to think it over. At break-time he returned and said, 'I'm sure it doesn't eat biscuits.' This boy, who was not yet an able reader, went into the corridor and looked through an encyclopaedia until he found a picture of a slow-worm. He got an older child to read the text to him and came back in triumph to tell his teacher, 'It eats worms!'

2.7   The slow-worm was kept in the school dining-room, with a notice beside it, written by the boy, saying, 'It only eats worms.' It gave rise to many writing and reading activities. One day it escaped from the tank and proved that it was not aptly named, so more notices were made: 'do not take the lid off', 'Do not touch', 'it moves very fast', and so on. Other labels proliferated, such as 'don't feed it', 'it bites', until the tank was surrounded by reading material.

2.8   In writing and reading instructions for pets, the pay-off for children is obvious and immediate: when the pets are properly looked after, they thrive; if they are not, they become ill and die. In the case of the budgies, the children's curiosity about finding the cage in an unusual place gave a strong motive for reading the explanation. How long would such a notice remain effectively interesting? Would you keep the same instruction manual long after the original children who wrote it had moved up the school? What other writing and reading activities could be generated by the presence of pets in the classroom? Would you introduce a creature like the slow-worm as a stimulus for reading and writing? Are you making the most of your guinea-pig? What would you do about incorrect spellings? What would you do about poor sentence construction?

3
'Sharon on Toast'

3.1 A typical after-dinner conversation in an infants' school on the south coast was the start of a series of reading and activities which finally involved the whole school. In this, as in most other infant schools, the daily menu is written up on a notice board in the corridor so the children know what they are going to have and often talk about it. This was a school with an unusually high standard of cooking, and enjoyment of that day's meal had led to a discussion of what everyone's favourite foods were—an inexhaustible and fascinating topic! It soon emerged that one child's meat was another child's poison.

3.2 This class of six-year-olds wanted to take their interest in food further. They collected different types of menu by reading the boards outside fish and chip shops and cafés on the way to school; they asked parents about restaurant menus and contributed suggestions from parties they had been to. Then they compared these menus with their daily fare at school.

3.3 With the help of some older children, they prepared a school survey by putting up a chart of the foods usually found on the dinner menu and getting all the pupils to tick which ones they liked and which ones they didn't. This was a very popular activity. Several children made the chart, some writing in the names of the food and others drawing and colouring pictures to go with them. This aid to word recognition, incidentally, insured that even the youngest infants knew what preferences they were expressing alongside difficult words like 'cauliflower' and 'shepherd's pie'.

3.4   When the chart had been up in the corridor for a few days and it seemed that everyone had filled it in, the children, again with the help of some older ones, organised the results into a new chart. They had to count the number of 'fors' and 'againsts' and then they listed each food in order of the preferences shown. Potatoes and carrots came out top, with green vegetables and onions well down the league-table! This second

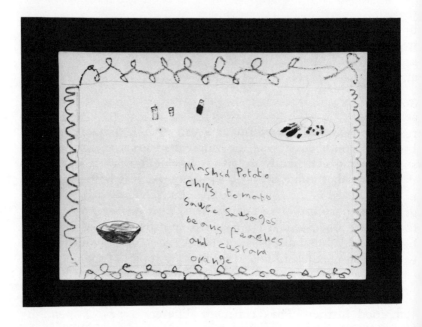

chart was also illustrated and put up in the corridor, so that the whole school could see the results of this very involving piece of market-research.

3.5   In this infant school, one child writes the dinner menu each day and decorates it in his or her favourite way. (Jelly and fish are the two most popular subjects for illustration and the latter are usually portrayed as goldfish swimming in a bowl, in spite of the school being on the coast!) Two little girls, when they were supposed to be writing 'roast beef and yorkshire pudding' put up this menu:

tomorrow's dinner

Sharon on toast

+ Diane in custard

Everyone who passed read that menu very carefully, to Sharon and Diane's intense satisfaction.

3.6   As a result of the children's interest in compiling menus, writing up the day's dinner and conducting the survey, special requests were made to the cook for repetition of favourites, inclusion of new dishes, increased frequency of favourite menus and a decrease of the least popular ones. The teacher had alerted the cook to this possible result and, as there was good liaison between classroom and kitchen, she co-operated happily with the project. Now the children often know in advance when a favourite dinner is planned and write up forthcoming attractions alongside the day's menu.

3.7   This was a particularly rich set of writing and reading activities, involving as it did all members of the school in some reading that was of interest to them, and producing involvement between classes. As it happened, all this took place in an infant school of under two hundred children. Could it be successfully done in the junior school? In a large comprehensive? Was it a necessary part of the activities that the food was particularly good, or could there be similar activities in less gastronomically fortunate schools? Could the results of the preference survey be analysed in further ways that the children would find interesting and engaging?

4

Dishes of the World

4.1   More exotic menus than sausages and baked beans were involved in this example. It happened at the time of United Nations Day in a class of six- to seven-year-olds. There had been discussion about different countries and their customs, particularly those represented in class. It was a cosmopolitan classroom, with children from Greece, Italy, Yugoslavia, Hungary, Lithuania, Holland and Germany. In the course of the discussion, one usually very quiet Greek boy volunteered the information that his mother made marvellous biscuits covered with icing sugar. This started some enthusiastic swapping of descriptions of national dishes.

4.2   As a result, members of the class came up with recipes for:

> Greek biscuits
> Hungarian goulash
> Dutch stew with potatoes on top
> German potato cakes

The teacher encouraged them to take this idea further than the descriptive stage by actually making the dishes in school. The children themselves

– checked on the recipes with parents and wrote them out for others to read,
– bought and organised the necessary ingredients,
– cooked all the dishes,
– ate the results.

4.3   The writing out of a recipe, even for a dish you know well, is often a complicated task for an adult. It involves planning and ordering the stages of preparation and cooking, listing ingredients, which are often hard to spell, getting quantities and measures right and making sure that no vital information is left out. Here is what a nine-year-old wrote as a recipe for a typically British dish.

★ *Pork Pie*
Ingredies: $\frac{1}{2}$ lb minced pork, 4 oz butter,
            2 oz lade, salt and pepper.
First you role the mince around in a frying pan. And then you make pasty with the butter and lard and rap it round the meat into a pie and cook it and ate it.

Young ones might need a lot of help with the writing but, since the proof of the pudding is in the eating, there would be an immediate check on how effective the instructions were.

4.4   Could this type of writing/reading activity work for your class? Do you have a mixture of nationalities? Would this necessarily be the only lead-in to such activities? In what ways could the writing and reading involved in cookery be further developed?

5
Red-letter Days

5.1   Children in the reception class often come in with the news, 'Today is my Mum's birthday' and ask if they can make her a birthday card. This activity, involving coloured card or paper, paints, crayons, gummed paper cut-outs and so on, is very enjoyable and, in order for the result to be a proper birthday card, some writing is necessary. The language involved: 'Happy Birthday', 'many happy returns', 'love from John', is usually familiar even to small children from their own experience, though they may ask for help with the writing. Addressing the envelope for the card is another relevant part of an enjoyable, purposeful activity.

5.2   Mums' birthdays are not the only stimuli for this kind of writing and reading. Seasonal occasions like Christmas and Easter often produce the idea among children themselves that they would like to make cards. If a member of the class is ill at home or away in hospital, the making and writing of get-well cards and letters serve a real purpose, both for the recipient and for the rest of the class who may be worried about illnesses and hospitals.

5.3   One infant school set up a post-box in the corridor because the children wanted to post the cards they had made for one another and the teachers. This was a popular move which eventually gave practice for many reading and organisational skills, since the cards needed to be sorted and delivered. Some children made a rota for sorters and deliverers. The sorters first divided the cards up into the classes written on the envelopes, but then they found that they needed a further way of organising the post so they arranged the cards alphabetically by name in each class. Then the deliverers took each batch to the appropriate class and set them out on the teacher's desk in a separate pile for each letter of the alphabet.

5.4   This was a very enjoyable series of reading and writing activities which eventually involved the whole school. In order

Dear mark

I hope you are geting better
and i hope you are
goingto like it when you
you come out and I hope
you are likeing the cards and
we are enjoying our selvs
and I hope you will soon
be out of hospital love

from   Sharon Jackson.

to make the Christmas cards, children had to write greetings and messages and address the envelopes with the name and class of the recipient. Further reading and indexing skills were needed by the sorters and, for those who had to deliver the cards to the individual classrooms, reading the addresses was an immediately functional necessity. When children came to look for their post on the teacher's desk, they were again using indexing skills in knowing which pile would contain their names. This particular school tried having the post-box as a permanent feature for children to post notes and letters to one another but, once the novelty had worn off, the flow of communications stopped and as many crisp-packets and chocolate-wrappers were posted as letters! Now the post-box is reserved for seasonal use only, Christmas, Easter and at the end of the school year, when children who are moving up into the junior school often write goodbye notes to their infant teachers.

5.5   Occasions like birthdays, whether of parents or members of the class, provide a good opportunity for children to explore time and develop planning concepts. One of the things I had expected to find in infant classrooms was a wall-diary, made by the children, to include all their birthdays and perhaps those of members of their families. Making such a diary, as well as being fun, would provide purposeful writing and reading activities, while helping to teach the days of the week, the months of the year and so on. So far, I have not come across such a calendar, but it seems a useful way to practise the idea of looking ahead and planning in advance when to make cards and so on. If the birthdays of the mums and dads and brothers and sisters are included, there should be no week in the school year without its red-letter day to involve someone in reading and writing for a functional purpose.

5.6   Is this kind of activity best suited to the infant class-room? Could it be adapted for use with older age groups? The value of a diary for birthdays as an introduction to planning ahead has been suggested; are there other types of diary or calendar that could have similar uses? The sending and receiving of post of all kinds, pleasant and unpleasant, is very much part of an adult's life. How can the children in your class be intro-duced to this means of communication?

6

Writing about Reading

6.1   In a school in south-east England, where there is a well-used book-corner, the writing of book reviews is a frequent activity. This particular school is lucky in having a very inviting area in what used to be a cloakroom, which has been redecorated by parents and provided with comfortable places to sit. Pre-school children come in with their parents to the story-telling sessions which the head teacher runs; it is well stocked with interesting books and is often busy with children. Books are often discussed in school and when a child expresses a strong preference or dislike of a particular story he or she is encouraged to write it down, so that it can be put up in the book-corner to help other children decide whether the story would appeal to them.

6.2   These reviews are not limited to the books which can be found in school. As one little girl says firmly at the end of her review of *Snow-White and Rose-Red*, 'I read the book at home and it is my own book.' Another enthusiast remarks, 'I am going to buy this book for myself next time I go out,' which is the strongest recommendation possible. Consider this review of *The Three Little Pigs*, by a six-year-old: 'I like The Three Little Pigs because it ends with a happy ending and the wolf gets kiled and the three little pigs live in peace I like the bit when the wolf coums down the chimmey and the last pig puts a pot of water at the bottom of the chimmey and it was too hot for the wolf and He gets killed and that was that and the three little pigs live happly ever after.' Writing a review is a complex task, involving planning and selection and a balance between telling the story and giving an opinion. The little girl who wrote about the three pigs managed this quite well, although she did give away the ending! She had also noticed and used the convention of giving words in titles an initial capital, quite observant for a child whose only other concession to punctuation was a final full stop.

6.3   This is a school which holds an assembly at the end of the day after the afternoon break. The assembly always has a specific theme, and on the day I visited them, half a dozen children read their own reviews of their favourite books. Those who had chosen existing books just told the story but, interestingly enough, several children when asked to write about their favourite or 'best' book had decided that none of those available lived up to this designation. So they had written their own stories, which they read out to the others. There was a strong tendency for the heroines of these stories to have the same name as their author and the action to consist of a series of meetings with talking cats and dogs, but they met with no less appreciation from the younger children listening than the adventures of Red Riding Hood and Peter Pan.

6.4 With older children, more experienced with reading and writing, reviewing books could become a more sophisticated activity. The way to judge the effectiveness of any review is to see whether the reader has gained an impression of the content and style of a book and its appeal to that individual. The criticisms of other children would be valuable in helping the reviewer to make all these points. If several children were reviewing the same book the resultant discussion would be a good introduction to literary criticism for older pupils.

6.5 The reading and writing activities described in this section came from a school in which an emphasis is placed on books and reading. The children are not from particularly highly literate homes—there is a considerable social mix of agricultural and industrial workers and some members of professions in the catchment area—but books are an accepted part of the school's daily life. How could a single teacher in a school not so well provided with a book area develop this source of functional reading and writing activities? What further could be achieved as the result of children deciding to write their own 'best' books? Is the writing of reviews useful only for works of fiction, or could information books be assessed in the same way? If reviews are written, are they just pinned up for a while in the book-corner, or is there any class discussion about differences in opinion? What else besides books could profitably be dealt with by this kind of written assessment to be read by others? What aspects of adult life will these skills be helpful for?

7
A Christmas Carol

7.1   Christmas was coming and a class of six-year-olds was preparing for a concert to be given for parents. The group was discussing what was to be performed and, in addition to all the traditional repertoire, it was suggested that they sing an Italian carol because there was an Italian child in the class. Lydia went home and learned a carol from her mother, which she later put on to the tape recorder. The words of the carol were written down by Lydia, whose first language was English, in an approximation to Italian which she could read back. Equipped with the tape recording and her transcription of the words, Lydia began to teach the class to sing it.

Soon all the children wanted to have the words and a group wrote them out and ran off cyclostyled copies for all the others. From then on until the day of the concert, the class members carried the words of the carol with them and often practised with the taped tune.

7.2   In most infant schools, some music is taught for voice or recorder. This is itself a form of functional reading, since it introduces a system of written conventions whose various characteristics, such as bar lines, phrasing, tied notes and so on, have their equivalents in written language. For a child standing in front of a sheet of music with his recorder, to be able to read the notes is all part of playing the instrument. Unfortunately, it is rare to find a school where children write out tunes for each other, but this quite easy activity would aid the writing skills used in language too.

7.3   Does music play an important part in your school? Do you use it to back up reading and writing activities in language work? Are there any children in your class who, while not progressing in reading, are able to follow a line of music? Do any of your poor readers play a musical instrument? If music is not one of your specialities, a short session with a colleague would be enough to suggest ways of using the analogy. What further activities could arise, involving reading and writing, from such musical examples as given above (7.1)?

8

Getting it Taped

8.1 Many infant schools now have tape recorders. The method of operating a cassette machine is particularly well suited for younger children to use. Children at Dymchurch School wanted to make an 'entertainment programme', to put through the school's loud-speaker system as if on radio. Some of the children knew how to use the recorder, but many others were uncertain. As in the guinea-pig example (2.2), it became clear that it would be more useful to have the instructions written down for everyone to consult. So one child wrote down the simple procedures in his own language, with suggestions from others, and the instruction card was kept with the recorder. In this particular example there was further reading and writing involved in the preparation and delivery of scripts for the radio programme and many classes were involved.

8.2 The cassette recorder was used for many purposes in this school. Often stories were recorded on to a small cassette library, so that a child could find and hear them when he wanted. Here is one instruction card made by a six-year-old:

1 press ̄on ̄ button
2 check that lights on
3 press start button
4 ghost stories begain at 008
5 to stop press stop bar
6 to turn tape back press Rewind button and stop it just before 008
7 to listen put ear phone on then press start

8.3 In another school, the arrival of a number of new audio-visual aids had made children and teachers concerned for the safety of the new equipment. One child in a class of seven-year-olds suggested that they should have a licence to operate each

piece of equipment, 'like Mum and Dad had to drive a car.'
Their teacher agreed to duplicate a licence if the children worked
out what should be on and what qualifications would be needed
to get a licence. A group of children started work on this
enthusiastically and gradually involved the whole class. Different children worked out the user requirements for each piece
of equipment; an example follows.

8.4   *SONY TC 100 Tape Recorder*
> 1 The on/off switch looks like this ⬚ on off
>   It is on the right of the recorder at the front.
> 2 The pause switch is on the left near the front.
>   It looks like this ⟨⟩
>   You need to push it forward to use it.
> 3 To record you need Sony microphone no. 1 and it is
>   plugged into the hole marked *mic*
> 4 It is a reel to reel tape so you need to have a tape on a
>   reel and a spare reel.
>   It is threaded from the right reel to the left reel.

> Like this. ◯ ⬚ ◯

> You have to be able to
>   Thread it up
>   Switch it on
>   Start it
>   Pause it
>   Stop it
>   Wind it back
>   Record with it

The licence prepared for users of this machine was made like
this:

FRONT	BACK
Licence no_____	I can
Name_____	Thread it up
is licensed to operate	Switch it on
Sony TC100	Start it
Signed_____	Pause it
	Stop it
	Wind it back
	Record with it

8.5   Given the situation described in 8.3, what modifications would you make in your class? Could the children, who
were so enthusiastic about their licence project, have been
further involved in meaningful reading and writing activities?
Who do you think should sign the licence to use the equipment?
Audio-visual aids are sometimes thought of as usurping the
reading and writing functions of traditional materials, but these
examples show that this need not be the case. Can you devise
ways of using your audio-visual equipment to promote reading
and writing which will be easily recognised as relevant by your
class?

9

Teaching the Teacher

9.1   This is an example of a single child who came to see the
point of writing and reading. He was six and a half, the youngest
of a family of four, whose mother was worried that he was not
working at school. Mark could read, but only when he wanted;
most of the material his teacher had tried held no interest for
him. One day when Mark's mother and teacher were talking,
it emerged that he was fascinated by cars and knew 'everything'
about them. This gave his teacher, who was taking driving
lessons at the time, an idea. She mentioned within Mark's
hearing that she found it very difficult to remember where
everything was in her car and what the various parts were for.
Later on the same day, Mark came up and offered to explain
it all to her. At lunch-time he carried out his promise and his
teacher says, 'I really believe he could have driven that car.' At
the end of this session Mark's teacher thanked him for his help,
but pointed out that she might have forgotten his explanations
before her next driving lesson. After giving it some thought,
Mark offered to write the instructions for her if she would help
him with the hard words.

9.2   He was as good as his word and wrote everything down
for her use. Every week, after her driving lesson, he would ask
the teacher how far she had got and write down the next stage of

instructions for her. If it had not been for the conversation with Mark's mother, his teacher would never have suspected the specialised knowledge of this six-and-a-half-year-old, which resulted in his writing to such a relevant purpose. Are any of your poor readers like Mark? Do you know if they have specialist knowledge or interests? What further reading and writing activities could have resulted from this situation? How would you have connected the car-instructions with Mark's class work, to continue to capture his interest?

10

Labels and Wombles

10.1   Everyday school and classroom tasks offer ideal opportunities for furthering writing and reading. The making of labels, lists, rotas and captions provides tasks within the competence of the youngest beginning reader which give great satisfaction when they are seen to fulfil necessary functions in the organisation of the classroom. Some infants in a school I visited had decided that the label on the caretaker's cupboard was no longer legible and that they would make him a new one. They also decided to label their lavatories 'boys' and 'girls' to help visiting and new children—a very functional activity! This was a school where the children in the end labelled every door, including the staff conveniences which they called 'Ladies' and 'Gentleman', on the grounds that there was only one male teacher! Rotas were very much a part of the daily organisation of this school, one of the most important being the 'wombling' rota. (If there is any reader left who does not know what Wombles are and what they do, I should explain that they are furry creatures, invented by children's writer Elizabeth Beresford; they live under Wimbledon Common and wage war on litter. 'To womble' = to pick up rubbish.) Other rotas are made for looking after pets, writing up the day's dinner menus and sorting and tidying classroom materials.

10.2   Another probable stimulus for writing and reading in school tasks is the chaos which follows certain classroom activities. If everyone is knee-deep in paper and Plasticine and yoghurt cartons, there is good reason to discuss the ordering and division of tasks, again involving children in the important strategies of planning. Tidying materials away is made easier by their proper places being labelled, and if the children have made their own labels, so much the better. Instructions for looking after pets and plants and equipment, as mentioned in previous examples (2.8), are also part of regular classroom tasks, as are those for mixing paints, paste and other materials. More occasional writing is also involved in making labels for objects on nature tables, and elsewhere—for example, 'I found this bird's egg on my nan's garage floor. Please do not touch it.'

10.3   There are many infant classrooms in which labels are used profusely without any apparent function. 'Window', 'blackboard', 'cupboard', 'sink' and so on would seem to be superfluous, when even the smallest child knows what all these things are. It is easy to understand the teacher's reasons for having this kind of label; they are probably connected with her concern to provide an environment in which examples of written language, from one word upwards, are abundant and to familiarise the children with the configuration of words. As a way of providing practice in acquiring the *skills* of reading, it is a laudable intention; what it does not do is introduce any ideas to children about what reading is for or why there is any need to learn to do it. In the same way, if pencils and scissors and rulers are kept in tubs and cartons which make the contents clearly visible, children do not need to refer to the label in order to find what they need. If, however, your classroom system stores materials in drawers or sliding trays on racks, the writing and reading of labels becomes a crucially relevant activity. And if the children, rather than the teacher, make the labels, they will learn a lot about the necessity for large clear lettering in a display context. I have not yet come across a teacher brave enough to start off with a completely language-free environment and build up a language-rich one from the needs of the children as they arise. It would obviously be less convenient in a teaching situation than having everything systematically arranged and docketed, but I was surprised that no one had actually tried it.

10.4   I once visited a flat rented by two student teachers, in which they had put Letraset labels on every fixture and fitting, saying 'light-switch', 'wash basin', and so on. Examining your

own classroom from this perspective, do you find many examples
of 'reading for reading's sake' to justify this kind of ironic comment on British infant school practice? Is there such a thing as a
classroom environment *too* rich in reading material? Are there,
on the other hand, items of equipment, or places of storage, which
could usefully carry labels and instructions, but don't? Is the
effectiveness of labelling limited to those children who have
carried it out? How long would you leave up labels before getting
them replaced and re-made by other children? Who makes
rotas in your classroom for regular tasks? Can you think of
further aspects of regular school and classroom tasks which
would generate functional reading and writing?

I I

Something to Look Forward to

11.1   As well as school tasks, school events are often a highly
motivating source of reading and writing activities. Jumble
sales, festivals, parents' evenings and plays can all generate
invitations, announcements, advertisements and letters directly
related to some immediate need. Here is a letter written by one
child to a local tradesman:

★ Dear Mr Cobb
Will you save some old shoe boxies For our harvest festival
please because we want to put our harvest gifts into them for
the old people
              Adrian   /

He received back a letter from Mr Cobb on business paper,
addressed to him personally at the school, promising him the
boxes that were needed. In writing this letter and reading the
reply, Adrian was having a good introduction to one functional
aspect of adult life and getting the prompt feedback which makes
this kind of activity valuable.

11.2   Adrian's school was having a jumble sale and wanted
to make a printed notice for all the children to take home to
parents. Two six-year-olds started writing drafts and, using the

best of their ideas, came up with a final version which was printed:

> ★ Please Come to the JUMBLE SALE at the INFANTS' SCHOOL on SATURDAY, 18th March at 2.30 pm
> There will be fantastic bargains to buy: books, toys and clothes. Come and meet your friends and have a cup of tea with them. Make it an afternoon out.

The spelling and punctuation was the teacher's, but the phrases were the children's own. There had to be discussion about what it was necessary to include as factual information as well as providing incentive for people to come. When the jumble sale took place there was more writing for children making price-tags, labels and notices. Since visitors were coming into the school, directional arrows and other signs were also made. On larger occasions, when people were expected to be coming from a distance, maps of how to find the school have been made.

11.3   At Dymchurch School, near Folkestone, a school event took place which was absorbingly interesting to the children. One of their teachers had left to have a baby and when her new son was still very young, she arranged with the local Rector to have him christened in the school, with all the children present. As the day came near there were great preparations, a christening cake was made by the children and, as it had three tiers, several classes co-operated to produce it. Following a recipe is a very functional reading activity and, although the children did not get the usual immediate reward of eating the cake then, they were very excited about the prospect of eating it at the christening party. Some wrote anticipatory accounts; from the short but triumphant

> ★ On Friday I am going to Gareths christening orange juice and me might sit on chairs,

to detailed enthusiasm:

> ★ at school Gareth is getting christened on Friday and we are going to the christening and so are some of the Mummys and DaDDys coming and the vicar does get some watter from the font and springcoll some on the Head and does a cross and after the christening we have a party and we have orange juice and he does cut the christening cake and we all have a bit and it Has aising on the Top.

The event took place and was as interesting to the children as they had hoped. They sang songs which they had learned beforehand, which had involved reading the words and learning them.

11.4   After the event, the Rector wanted a report of it in his Parish Magazine so ten children from the school wrote one for him. Each child wrote an individual report and they all then discussed which items from each should be included. Surprisingly to their teacher, many of the first drafts contained items unique to that writer, so that sorting out of materials in the discussion was not too difficult. With some help from the teacher, the children selected the contributions and noted what order they should come in. They were in fact editing their own materials into a final draft, which was then copied out by one of the group. Here are some extracts from the final report which was published in the magazine.

★ Mrs Jones had her baby Christened in this school because most of the children had not seen a Christening and Mrs Jones used to be a teacher here and some of us were in her class . . . Mr Rotherwell's Class and Mrs Gallagher's Class and Mrs Gibbon's Class made the Christening Cake. It was three big cakes on top of each other and it said 'Gareth David' on the white icing in blue icing. It tasted good . . . Gareth wore a white dress and it was the one his Grandmother was Christened in.

11.5   Gareth's christening was an unusual event and it is unlikely to find a parallel in many primary schools, but the reading and writing connected with it were interesting to the children for many reasons. Continuity with their teacher who had recently left was of prime importance; it not only established another link between the school and the community but allowed the children to become involved with the result of the pregnancy they had partly observed. The reading of recipes for making the christening cake had an interesting pay-off in the not-too-distant future, as did the learning of songs for the occasion. Writing a report for the magazine was a perfectly usual procedure, which the children could see the point of. Having to organise their impressions and recollections of the occasion gave excellent planning opportunities which were well used.

11.6   There are always events in the school year which bring in members of the local community or take children out into it. It would be a useful activity to make a calendar of all such events, containing descriptions and perhaps reminders of dates by which jumble, money, and so on should be brought. A termly rather than—or as well as—a yearly calendar would be a good introduction to planning and organising a conceivable time span. Perhaps a weekly bulletin might be drawn up by each class from the larger over-all calendars, but a rota would probably be needed to keep up such a regular commitment. I have seen no examples of such school or class diaries as yet, but they seem a good preparation for the organisation and allocation of time in adult life. Have you anything like this in your classroom? What writing, reading, and in particular, planning activities involved with school events can be encouraged which the children will recognise as relevant?

Part 2

Junior and Middle School

12

Sowing and Growing

12.1   In an Outer London suburb, a class of first-year juniors carried out a systematic series of reading and writing activities generated by their own interests. One child came into school with some runner beans and peas and asked to grow them. There were enough to share round among the twenty-nine children in the class and there was lively discussion about ways of growing them. They decided to plant some in pots with soil and some in jam jars with blotting-paper and water. When this was done they wanted to record the day of planting so that they could see how long it took for the plants to grow. Because they were worried that some children might forget to water their plants and others water them too often, they worked out, through trial and error, which days to water them and then wrote out notices to remind one another.

When the plants began to grow, a race between plants developed, which entailed some strict rules which the children wrote down. They measured the beans—the peas didn't grow fast enough—and recorded their growth rate each week. Details of how and when to measure were written down by them for one another to read. When the plants started to take over the classroom—they reached the top of the blackboard—the holidays arrived, and they were carefully carried home, together with the growth charts and booklets the children had written.

12.2   Another junior school teacher pointed out to me some more of the many reading, writing and planning activities involved in growing plants. She suggested that children who want to grow things could first read a seed catalogue, which is usually brightly illustrated and attractive. When they have planned what flowers they want to grow, they can write the order form themselves and send for the seeds. Each seed packet has to be read for specific planting details and there are many opportunities for diagrams of seed beds and flower-colours, charts of planting-times, and similar activities.

When it comes to planting time, distances between rows and seeds have to be measured according to instructions, as does the depth at which the seeds are planted. Later on, when the seedlings are ready to be planted out, more instructions have to be read. A record of planting dates and expected flowering dates needs to be made and labels written for each row of seeds. This teacher ended by adding that since any children who read instructions so carefully and kept such accurate records could expect a bumper crop, more writing would then be needed for advertisements to sell the surplus!

12.3   Infant school teachers are also familiar with children bringing in everything from seeds to conkers into school and asking if they will grow. One teacher always asks the children what *they* think plants need in order to grow and lets them discover by experiment and evaluation. Most of the children volunteer water but there is always discussion about how much, a little or a lot, and how much is a lot? They perhaps water one pot with 20 cups a day, one with 10, one with none, according to the children's own suggestions. In order to find out how the experiment is working, they need to keep records about quantities and frequency of watering, hours of light and dark, heat, soil, depth of planting, and so on. Growth charts are also kept and there is an important evaluation stage when the children decide which ways have worked best and which they would use again for what kind of plant. At this stage they compare their own findings with gardening books and magazines brought from home and the instructions on commercial seed packets.

12.4   The activities involved in planting and growing are varied and enjoyable, and the reading and writing develops naturally as part of the practical situation. The pay-off in watching the plants grow is gradual but satisfying. Flowers bring their own kind of interest in colours and scents, but some vegetables are quite easy to grow, and children could have the added satisfaction of eating at least their own potatoes. If land cannot be spared or found outdoors, there are still many opportunities for growing plants indoors.

What further sorts of reading and writing activity might evolve from sowing and growing? What other forms of planning and recording could be used?

13
Playing the Game

13.1   Christmas and birthdays often result in children bringing complicated games and construction kits to school. One
teacher of a remedial group told me that often after Christmas
the children were playing elaborate board games quite wrongly
because neither they nor their parents could read the instructions. It does not help that the rules for these games are usually
given in very small print and often use long, unfamiliar words.
However, the desire to play the attractive and mysterious game
which has been given as a present is a strongly motivating force.
Many of the games, like *Cluedo*, involve reading cards or instructions as part of the play; others, like *Scrabble*, are based on
dexterity with words and require some spelling skills. Construc-
tional kits and models are other popular presents which demand
some reading as well as mechanical ability.

13.2   One possible way of handling this situation used by one
teacher is to take a game whose rules are unfamiliar to you and to
your class and try to work out how to play it without looking
at the instructions. A knowledge of certain play conventions,
like card-dealing, dice-throwing, progress round a board,
penalties, is a help to understanding, which the children may
not yet have acquired. These conventions may be elicited by
asking the class what games they already know and what you do
to play those. With most games it is not possible to work out all
the rules without reading either the instructions or the writing
on the board or playing equipment. Four years ago I was given
a Chinese game consisting entirely of little counters with patterns of dots and pictures on them. It came from a Chinese
shop and had no English instructions; I am still trying to work
out how to play it! Although this is less the case with construction kits like *Meccano*, it is difficult to put complicated models
together if you can't follow the instructions.
  The point of this teacher's exercise is not just to show that the
instructions are necessary, but to get the class to work out what

sorts of things they need to know about the game. In this way, they have certain expectations—a 'mental set'—which will aid word and phrase perception. They produce the vocabulary, which they then stand a better chance of recognising when they turn to the instructions. At the end of this attempt to work out the game, when the children have produced all the likely words and attempted to spell them, and when they have worked out what types of instructions are necessary (for instance, how many players? How are the moves made—by throwing dice, moving counters, or in other ways? In what order do the players move?), the teacher gets out the booklet, which she has had photocopied, and the class match their expectations with the rules provided. The pay-off here is simple but satisfying; they play the game.

13.3 One particular infant school teacher begins to train this ability to anticipate patterns by getting her children to tell her the rules of their playground games. As well as the traditional playground games with their long and fascinating history, presented in the work of Iona and Peter Opie, every school has its own *ad hoc* made-up games. These are often difficult for an adult to follow—like 'Chalky Tara', a game which three children (one called Tara) demonstrated to me. They passed a piece of chalk rapidly back and forth among the three and when someone called 'Stop!', the child holding the chalk would be greeted by cries of 'Chalky Tara!' (or whatever the child's name was), followed by fits of giggles. This game could be played with any object, they explained, only then you had to change the name to 'Grapefruit Tara', or whatever.

This is just the sort of invented game often played repeatedly without boredom which the infants teacher watches in the playground. She observes it in action for some time and then suggests

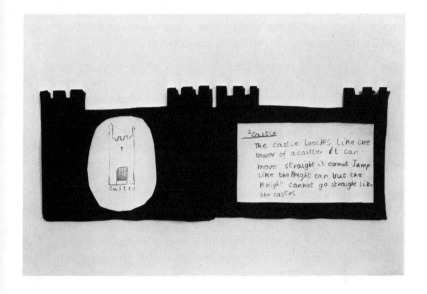

that others might like to learn how to play it. The players/inventors are usually willing to write down the instructions to be stored for use at any time. In order to do this there has to be consultation, perhaps playing through the game and noting what is done at each point. When the children have reached a first version, some others who have not as yet played run through it following the instructions, while the authors watch. Any necessary modifications are made then and the rules are kept where other children can read them and use them either to play that

game or to generate ideas for new games of their own. A group
of children in this school made an instruction booklet for how
to play chess, illustrating the pieces and describing the possible
moves.

13.4   In a primary school in the north of England there was
a very keen netball team, which eventually won the League
Championship. The girls discussed the game within school and
outside and one day came to ask the teacher if she had any books
on netball. She lent them the only book she had on the subject
and they extracted the relevant parts for each member of the
team. Each player had some written information about her
position and movements in the game. When the girls had
finished with their teacher's book, they moved on to borrowing
books on netball from the public library and continued their
researches in order to improve their game.

13.5   There is an obvious link with adult roles in all these
examples; leisure activities are a part of most adult lives and
sometimes form the most highly motivated of all, since they are
voluntarily undertaken. But as well as preparing for the use of
adult free time, the following of instructions for games is of
value in learning to follow any series of stepped rules or procedures. If you can follow ordered stages for making a model of a
vintage Rolls Royce car, you may also be able to follow the rules
for lighting a gas boiler, or the safest procedures during a fire.
Are there further ways in which games can be used to stimulate
writing and reading activities? How would you use the situations
described in this section? Would you follow the method of the
teacher in 13.2? With what age groups could you use games as a
spur to reading and writing?

14

The Young Consumers

14.1   I have drawn the examples in this section together
because of their clear link with the adult role of consumer. In
some of them the idea was initiated by the children themselves,
in others by the teacher, but in all cases the items under discus-

sion were a part of the children's everyday familiar experience and reading and writing about them was seen as a relevant activity.

In a group of third and fourth years at a junior school in the home counties, there was a very popular purchase among the children which I shall refer to as a 'Lucky Dip Bag'. For 2p, a bag offered some sweets, novelties and a card, and several children in the group had recently found that the sweets were stale and some of the toys broken. They brought their complaint to the teacher who said, 'Well, what are you going to do about it?' After much discussion, they decided to write a letter of complaint to the manufacturer, but they agreed that they needed to do some more research before writing the letter. One possibility was that the local retailer had had the goods in her shop too long so, as well as buying some more bags from the village shop, the children also bought some supplies from shops in the nearest large town. In the course of their survey they discovered that the manufacturer's name and address has to be printed on packaging in case customers are dissatisfied with the goods. They also learned the meaning of such words as 'novelty' (in this context) and 'confectionery', and they discovered the variation in the contents—for example, 'I found a Badminton and 5 sweets and a small packet of sweets', 'I found three small tanks and 17 different sweets.' The children also wrote down what else they could buy for the cost of a Lucky Dip Bag: sherbert fountains; a bar of animal chocolate; a packet of football cards; five pieces of bubble gum; a packet of car stamps. When their survey was complete, the children extracted the main points and discussed and planned their letter. As a result they received a letter of apology from the manufacturer together with a free supply of Lucky Dip Bags in good condition.

14.2 Another group in a junior school in Hertfordshire decided to do a 'best buy' survey on different brands of crisps. This was half a class of nine- to ten-year-olds, described by their teacher as 'very bright'. They found the *Which?* report on crisps and included it in the folder they were making, for comparison with their own findings. They bought examples of six brands, including the 'own-brands' of some supermarkets, and made tables of weights and prices. Also listed were the ingredients, which produced some unexpected ones like 'permitted

anti-oxidant', and the order of difficulty involved in opening the
packets.

★ Some were harder than others to open, but we never
needed a knife or scissors though Terry said we ought to have
a hammer and chisel ready just in case.

When they had been through all these stages, their teacher put
out some crisps from each packet into identical bowls, without
identifying them except to herself, and the children tasted and
passed verdict on the brands of crisp. Here are some of their
conclusions:

★ Out of the twelve of us, nine thought the crisps were 'just
right' with the salt and three thought they weren't salty
enough. Nobody thought they were too salty.
★ We don't like the dark old potato skins left on our crisps.
These look horrid and put you off. It was hard guessing which
flavour was which when we didn't have the bag to tell us.
★ We don't like the way X put the weight of their crisp in
drams and grams where everybody else uses ounces. This
means that it is not easy to compare the crisps where you get
most for your money.

This survey taught the group of enthusiastic crisp-consumers
a lot about estimating the value and quality of goods offered for
sale and required them to write out tables and to read weights,
ingredients and prices; they were learning to use the basic
reading/comparing/evaluating skills necessary for the discern-
ing consumer.

14.3   Another consumer project involved that perennial
favourite, baked beans. Two junior groups carried out comparative surveys like the crisp one. They were nine-year-olds, a
group of eleven in each case, but the projects took place a year
apart with the same teacher. She described the second group as
'less able' than the first, but thought that the project had suc-
ceeded much better the second time round. Of course, this was at
least partly due to the teacher's evaluation of what she had done
with the first group and the improvements she made before trying
it with another. With the first group, she had written a questionnaire on the blackboard, which the children used as the basis
for their sampling and judgments, but the second group made
their own questionnaire, themselves deciding what questions

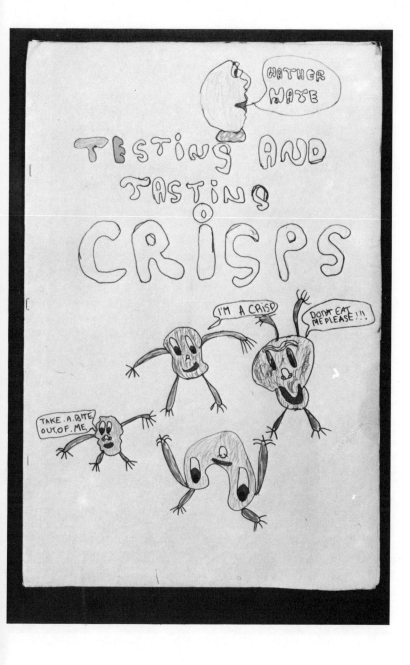

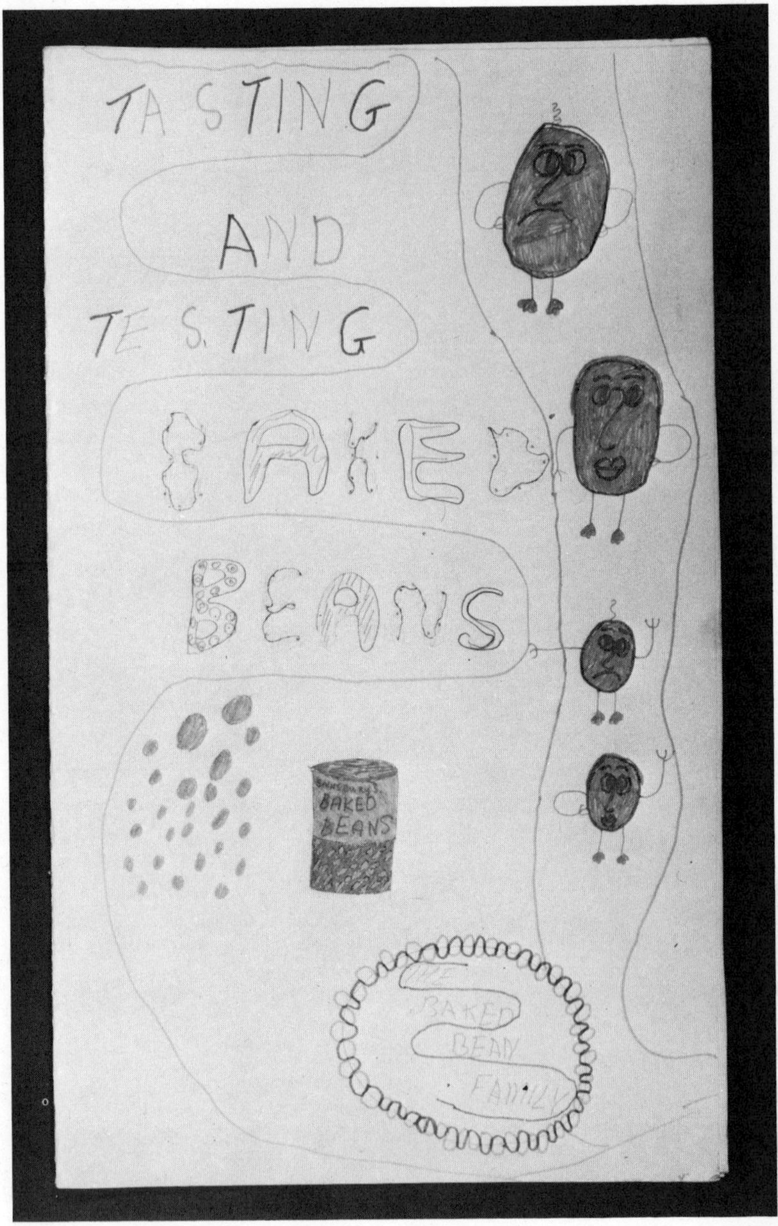
TASTING
AND
TESTING
BAKED
BEANS
BAKED BEANS
BAKED BEAN FAMILY

needed to be asked. The first survey nevertheless unearthed some interesting facts:

★ Do you know that different brands of baked beans contain different things? All have beans, tomatoes and sugar, but only some have *onions*. One even has *milk*.

★ Some people think that baked beans are raw and that they need cooking before you eat them.

This last emerged because one mother objected to her child 'eating raw beans' during the tasting!

The second group described their methods:

★ We bought nine different kinds of baked beans so that we could find out which was the best value for the money and which we liked best. First, we looked carefully at the tins and made a table showing weights and prices. Then we looked at the labels on the tins, and we found that the ingredients varied. Secondly, we opened the tins and found that the colours were different, some being red and others brownish. Some of the tins had much more sauce than the others. Then we tasted the beans and said which one we liked best. The tins were numbered 1–9.

They made charts of comparative weights and prices, and ingredients and graphs of 'the brand we like the most', 'the

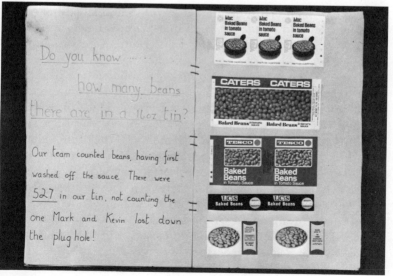

brand we liked the least' and 'which we thought looked the sauciest' and bound them into a folder. Apart from the initial idea, which came from the teacher, they had planned the whole survey themselves.

14.4   The junior consumer project which involved the most reading was definitely the one on comics. This was undertaken by a group of mixed ability children, aged between ten and eleven, who had been left out of a school canal trip. They had chosen six topics for a consumer-type survey and had a week in which to complete them. They rounded up all the different comics available in their local town on that first Monday morning; they found some thirty available, designed to appeal to pre-school children, infants, juniors, pre-teens and comic-buying parents. Their specific aim was to assess and collate the personal preferences of the team, to relate these to the preferences of their brothers and sisters, and finally to carry out a popularity poll amongst the rest of the school. (At this point they started pretending that they were a Gallup poll taking a sounding of public political opinions.) They were also eager to find out how much parental influence there was on choice, whether indeed children were free to spend their pocket money as they pleased, whether they were restricted because, 'Me Mum says it's just a load of trash.' Some of their findings and comments might well make producers and retailers think:

★ We think it is disgusting that Smith's and any other shops should sell old comics at the same price as new ones. They ought to be reduced as they get old. Some were a month out of date.
★ We all like to keep our comics in a collection or pass them on to other people. It is silly for paintings and competitions and cut outs and membership coupons for clubs to be on the other side of something important like a serial or a story. Why can't there be just advertisements on the other side?
★ We don't think that things for you to paint in comics are a good idea because the paper is too thin for you to paint properly because it goes all blotchy.
★ We thought that the print in little children's comics was too small for anyone learning to read . . . In older children's comics, capital letters were often used. We didn't like this, and we didn't like words spelt wrongly such as 'crook' spelt with a k.

★ We think that those with only a coloured cover and just black and white inside are a bit of a cheat.

At the end of the survey it was interesting to find that all the children in the team had switched their personal preferences now that they had had the opportunity of seeing a fuller range. This is the reason they decided to add in their writing-up a classification of the comics available, their prices, and some idea of the age groups for which they are suitable, so that parents and others might be urged to look around before making a decision.

14.5   These examples were all from the junior school. Could consumer projects be used to elicit relevant reading and writing activities in the infant school? Most of the goods surveyed were foods that are popular with children; they could be tasted as part of the survey and eaten as part of the tidying up afterwards. What pleasurable and engaging products could be studied other than food? What criteria would you use for conducting this kind of consumer project?

15
Smoke Signals

15.1   This next example also has a consumer element and it is certainly closely related to adult life. What prompted it was a concern of the children for their parents' health. Some very able children in their last year of junior school had seen the posters put out by the Health Education Council to discourage smoking and were worried because many of their parents smoked. There was the usual amount of surreptitious smoking by pupils in the school, but this particular small group—all boys—were worried about the link they had heard of between smoking and lung cancer. They not only were not tempted to try cigarettes themselves, but were also worried that their parents might get cancer. When their teacher heard about their fears, she thought the best way to handle the situation was for the children to investigate the facts themselves. She knew of the existence of a 'smoking man' model which inhales the smoke from a lighted cigarette and displays it entering and contaminating his lungs through his transparent torso. While she managed to get hold of this demonstration model, the boys found the *Which?* report on smoking (1971) which listed the relative tar and nicotine content of 25 popular brands of cigarette. They made a folder to contain all the information they could find on the subject and stuck in cigarette packets (which they collected from home) which didn't carry the government health warning, which proved that the retailers were selling stock which was several years old. One boy wrote out his own viewpoint to introduce the folder:

★ If you smoke you are likely to get cancer of the mouth throat or lungs.

A packet of cigarettes cost between 20 and 30p.

If you smoke 20 cigarettes a day you are likely to spend about £91.25 a year.

The government health warning says: smoking can damage your health.

French cigarettes do not have warnings.

Cigars are advertised on TV rather than cigarettes because they are more healthy.

Nicotine and tar are the most harmful parts of a cigarette. You can test these with a special man.

I have never tried a cigarette. I do not intend to smoke.

When they had demonstrated the model of the smoking man to all the rest of their class, the boys made a videotape about smoking which was shown at an open meeting for parents. This was the reverse of the usual situation in which parents try to discourage their children from smoking.

15.2   The boys involved in this activity had to do a lot of reading in order to extract the necessary information for their presentation of the subject to their class and to parents. They then chose to write up their findings. The reading and writing involved had as its aim the attempt to change parents' attitudes and practices; it represented a positive attempt to do something about what was on the children's minds. Are there other areas of health that might be worrying children which could be treated in this way? Do you think this is a proper topic for reading and writing activities? How would you have handled it? Do you think the teacher was right to introduce the life-like model and further negative information about smoking? If you were using such a subject, what further writing and reading could be involved that would be relevant?

16

Fasten your Seat-belts

16.1   This group of activities also originated with worries about the older generation. Some junior school children in a vertically grouped class had seen an item in a television programme about the necessity to wear safety belts. They had been rather surprised that so many of their parents had dismissed this as 'a load of rubbish' and wanted to know what the teacher thought. After some discussion about the merits and types of belt, it was decided to conduct a survey to find out how many people were actually wearing seat-belts, whether or not it was desirable. It was on an afternoon in summer when the class went down to the A41 with their note-books and pencils to check car-drivers and passengers as they stopped at the lights.

★ Between 2.00 and 2.15 pm yesterday our class went down to the A41. We watched the traffic and made records. Afterwards we made graphs. I made a graph to show how many people do and do not wear seat belts. Between 2.00 and 2.15 yesterday 29 people did wear seat-belts but 65 didn't. A lot of these people did have seat belts but just didn't wear them.

16.2   The class had been led on to discuss other aspects of safety for drivers before going down to the road, so another survey they did was on the colours of the cars they saw.

★ Out of all the colours of cars I saw white is the most popular and turquas is the least popular. White is the saffist colour to have because it glows up in the dark so people can see you better. Dark colours don't show up in the dark so that is a bit dangerous.

All the children who were recording car colours noted the correlation between popularity and safety in the case of white, but one or two noticed that colours like cream and bright yellow which are almost as safe were hardly represented. Their teacher was careful to point out to me that any type of survey involving some expensive consumer item like a car was far better carried out on a neutral site than by asking questions round the class. Nevertheless, several children volunteered facts about their family's car to compare with what they had found.

16.3   Preparation for the trip down to the A41 had led to a broader discussion about traffic than the original question of safety. As a result of talking about transport problems in this country, reduced parking space in the centres of towns and the private versus public transport debate, the children also wanted to count how many people there were in each car. This was one child's view:

> ★ Traffic control in London is terrible. They have yellow lines every were. They are thinking of taking all the parking meters down close all the car parks and stop cars coming in London they are saying that we will have to come to London by train or bus.

The reasons were given by another:

> ★ It is best that people give others lifts, which hardly anybody does as we found out when we went down to the motorway. We found that if anyone did have any more than one person in the car they were usually youngsters.

They found that 65 cars in their survey carried only one person, 20 carried two, 10 carried three and only 5 carried four.

16.4   Another topic which came under discussion was the proportion of British to foreign cars on the road and what made foreign cars appeal to British drivers. These were the findings and opinions of one child:

> ★ We went down to the A41 to see and count the British cars and the Foriegn cars. People buy Foriegn cars because they look more streamlined and because they get value for money and also you must 'KEEP UP WITH THE JONESES'. The most popular British car was the mini and the most popular Foriegn car was the Volkswagon.

What a lot he already knew about the vulnerabilities of the adult consumer!

These four aspects of traffic arose from the initial worry about safety belts. In diffusing the surveys to cover different areas, the teacher was helping to de-fuse some of the anxieties that the children were feeling. The larger issues of what factors to take into account when buying a car and the social and environmental implications of private car ownership arose naturally from the discussion and were helping the children towards mature decision-making as adult consumers. The members of this particular

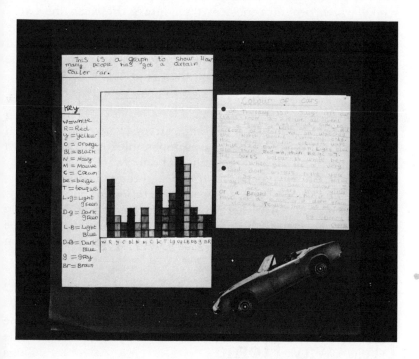

class were experienced car travellers and noticing makes and colours of cars was very much part of their daily life.

16.5 These were largely writing activities. Noting and recording skills were practised under high pressure and at top speed down by the motorway. Although the children were stationed at the lights, much of the traffic they observed was moving quite fast. When they returned to the classroom, they read back their notes and made graphs of their findings. Beside each graph was a description of what they had observed, sometimes with added information from their own experience. The children who had been involved in one branch of the survey read the results and looked at the graphs of the other three. The charts they made were then put up for other children in the school to look at and doubtless as another lesson for visiting parents.

16.6   Pupils in a school in south-west Hertfordshire launched a campaign of their own against a proposed motorway which threatened to separate their secondary school from the primary school which provides most of their intake. Between the two schools lies a beautiful tract of woodland used as the basis for environmental and rural studies in both schools. The children inundated the Minister for the Environment with letters, drawings, poems and posters. But their efforts, like those of the adults, failed and there is every likelihood that the motorway will go ahead, provided that the money can be found.

16.7   Would some kind of traffic survey project be relevant to the children in your school? It is impossible for anyone, even in the most rural areas of Britain, to be unaware of the problems connected with roads and traffic, and thinking about them while in the junior school is a good preparation for coping with them as an adult. Are there meaningful reading and writing activities connected with this aspect of everyday life which you could use with your children, capitalising on your local circumstances?

17

Fly Away Home

17.1   This is the story of a boy who was making no progress in reading until his teacher found material that had specific relevance to his own situation. Dave had just arrived from Jamaica, where he had been living with his grandparents, to join the parents he had not seen for three years; he was eight years old. He turned up at the local school in south-east London two days after the beginning of term and behaved quietly and amiably, but his teacher, who was new to the job, found him 'a problem and a challenge'. After reading through the first three *Ladybird Key Words* books (this was the series used by the school), he stuck at Book Four. Neither they, nor *Janet and John*, nor *Happy Venture*, which were also available in school, really 'suited his life style', as the teacher put it. Dave wasn't making friends in school and he seemed to be missing his family in Jamaica; he was becoming withdrawn and unhappy.

One day his teacher got Dave talking about 'home', what life was like in Jamaica, how it differed from life here, what he particularly missed and what things he liked about this country. The boy enjoyed their conversation and described the view of the sea from his grand-dad's house and the green bananas and yams so graphically that his teacher began to long to visit Jamaica. He suggested that Dave should make a book all about his country, to help remind him of his life there and for the other children to read, since he was sure they would be interested by the descriptions as he had been.

17.2 So Dave, who had previously read little and written less, made a book about Jamaica. The first pages were all about himself and his grandparents and their home and were just pictures with simple sentences underneath. He asked his teacher for most of the words he needed at the beginning and developed a trusting relationship with him. After a few more conversations, he wrote about the flight to England. By then he had become more confident and was making friends with the other children. The teacher, without exerting pressure, reintroduced him to the *Ladybird* scheme and this time Dave worked his way through Books Four, Five and Six. As he began to take an interest in other simple readers, his own book came to a halt through lack of material. There was nothing about Jamaica in either the school or the public library. Dave brought in some photographs from home and his teacher suggested that he should write to the Jamaican High Commission for some more illustrative material for his book. His language skills had improved so much by then that he was able to write the letter himself and he was delighted when a package of photographs and information booklets arrived from the High Commission. He stuck the illustrations into his book and wrote his own comments. By now he had reached *Ladybird* 8b and the stories were becoming more interesting to him; from then on until he reached the end of the series he would always ask to read if given the option.

17.3 Dave's teacher realised that his 'reading problem' involved emotional and social factors and took steps towards helping them all simultaneously. The boy's homesickness, and his need for material set in a life-style he could identify

with, were both met by his own book in his own language: 'his
great interest in his book not only gave him an interest in school
but in words.' There is a dearth of material relating to the
cultural and social needs of school children and reading primers
have long been under attack for presenting stereotyped situations and characters. Because reading schemes are both costly
and durable, the old-fashioned presentation and remote content
are still there in many schools as children's first introduction
to reading.

What is the situation in your class? Do you use a reading
scheme? If so, is its content really relevant to the children in
your class? Does the racial, sexual, social mix of the characters
in the stories bear any relation to the proportions in your classroom? If not, how would you adapt or replace the existing
materials to provide more relevant reading for the individuals
you teach?

18

Finders Readers

18.1   Another example of an individual child who developed
a relevant writing and reading activity took place in a British
Forces School in Italy. The teacher had a large old second-hand
book which she used a lot with her class. It had 767 pages and
was about sixty years old, containing fairy tales, nonsense
rhymes, limericks, fables, folk tales, children's classics, poetry,
and so on. The children in her class valued it for its fascinating
contents and knew that the teacher valued it too. But it was
tattered with age and lacked a contents page. Very often the
teacher would say, 'There's just the right story or poem to fit in
with today's weather', or 'this shell from the seaside' or 'that
cartoon that was on television last night', and then spent ages
leafing through the book to find the appropriate piece.

One ten-year-old girl became fed up with this inefficient
method and offered of her own accord to make a list of
contents for the book. Her teacher described her as 'only just
of average intelligence and her reading not highly efficient', but
she tackled this huge task and her contents list is now taped into

the front of the book where it has proved invaluable. Initially, she labelled her work INDEX and the teacher pointed out the difference to her between an index and a list of contents. As soon as she had finished the contents, she valiantly started on the next task, categorising the contents into stories, poems, fables, and other items. She was well on the way to understanding how to put an index together, when she had to leave that school. As her teacher points out, if the child could make her own table of contents and classify them, she was much better equipped to use other people's contents lists and indices. And all the while that she had the book in her possession and was looking through it for page-numbers and so on, this girl was in fact reading and re-reading it, to the improvement of her mechanical skills.

18.2 This introduction to a complex reading and writing task came about spontaneously at the child's own suggestion. She was obviously sufficiently interested in and rewarded by the material she was handling to complete the project she had undertaken and start on another, more complicated one. As her teacher implied, she was not a particularly likely pupil to want to do such work. Is there any way you can think of, without having the ready-made stimulus of the much-used book, to introduce children to the value of classifying and categorising material for storage and retrieval? How is the book-corner or junior library arranged in your school? Do children know how to find what they are looking for in these areas? Are there other resources besides books which could be helpfully classified in this way? How would you introduce children to the idea of classifying information as well as resources?

19
Looking It Up

19.1 The original activity described here was not really a 'guinea-pig' one at all, but it certainly has potentially guinea-pig characteristics! A teacher of third-year juniors in a mixed ability class found she needed extra activities for the half dozen or so of the thirty-five children who always finished their tasks in hand before the end of the lesson. She had made some work cards for the children to use with copies of the *Yellow Pages* classified telephone directory, simulating situations in which they would need to be consulted. For example:

> My washing machine has just flooded the kitchen floor. Please find me someone to help.
> I am an American visiting England and my daughter has got measles. Please find me a doctor.
> I am going away for my holidays and I would like some kennels for my dog near Kings Langley.

The children enjoyed the activity very much and there is no doubt that it linked with definite aspects of the adult role, connected with problem solving. But the teacher was the first to recognise how this could be more profitably developed.

19.2   She described to me how she would use the *Yellow Pages* again for reading and search activities. She would start with a class discussion about things that can go wrong in houses, perhaps starting with an example from her own recent experience. The class would all contribute incidents from their own lives when things had gone wrong in their houses. There would first be a discussion about how parents had actually gone about putting things right and getting repairs done and then the *Yellow Pages* would be introduced. Each child would look up the relevant service to deal with the problem or emergency he had just been discussing and there would then need to be further decisions made on the basis of the services available. Nearness of the firm, whether or not it ran a 24-hour service, whether it was billed as a special emergency service, what you could tell about the size or kind of the firm from its name and manner of presentation would all be factors to consider in making this kind of choice. Once this exercise had been accomplished and the children still had the *Yellow Pages* in their hands, the teacher would expand the idea of their usefulness from dealing with once-only emergencies to offering regular services, places of entertainment and so on. Since the *Yellow Pages* are organised like any other telephone directory, the children would not only be getting good practice in planning but would be getting familiar with the ways in which to look up a number.

19.3   A similar situation evolved in a comprehensive school when a girl wanted to know: 'Where can you take a suède coat

when you've dropped fish and chips on it?' Someone suggested
Yellow Pages and the girls all started looking up services they
might need. Many of them had never come across the *Yellow
Pages* before and were amazed at all the entries. How you could
receive it free and who paid for it were among the questions they
asked and they gradually acquired the knowledge that printed
materials were paid for by advertisements. When they looked
up hairdressers, they started to say things like, 'I wouldn't go
there; that's where that horrible Sandra works (an ex-school-
friend). I wouldn't let her near my hair!' They were already
assessing the neutral public information available in terms of
their subjective preferences.

19.4   The girls in the last example were getting close to the
stage where they could re-write their own *Yellow Pages* for a
smaller local area, giving more information about the comparative merits of firms and shops offering the same services and
goods. One class made a start on this when a girl found
advertised in the *Yellow Pages* a dry-cleaners which had
scorched one of her dresses a month before and had still not
dealt with the request for compensation which her mother had
made. 'Fast—Reliable', said the displayed advertisement in the
Yellow Pages and the girl took exception to its inclusion. After
that, other members of the class 'vetted' various sections in the
Pages and edited and annotated some of them for use as their
own personal directory in school. They noted which shops
pestered you to buy clothes and which let you look around in
your own time, which local cafés and restaurants slapped on a
substantial minimum charge at lunchtime or after 9.00 pm,
which hairdressers gave cut-price hairdos if you were willing
to accept a trainee and so on.

19.5   The personal *Yellow Pages* were not used for any wide
purpose in this particular case and the activity was not developed
beyond a single afternoon. In what ways could the children's
knowledge and experience of local shops and services be used to
provide information that was not only profitable and interesting
for them to compile, but also useful to others? How would you
handle the subjective element in passing judgment on some
particular local amenity?

Using the *Yellow Pages* is a good introduction to many aspects
of adult life. Problem-solving and use of the telephone direc-
tories have already been mentioned, but what is really being

developed is skill in using an index or any other classification
system which uses alphabetical order. Can you think of further
writing or reading activities connected with an information
resource like the *Yellow Pages*?

20

A Koala-bear Activity

20.1   This next example comes from Australia but there is
no reason why it shouldn't find equivalents in this country.
Since I have not yet come across one of this type that was
as good, I think it worth including as an antipodean 'guinea-
pig'.

The Festival of Arts in South Australia, as my correspondent
writes, is a very important event and is given a lot of time on TV
and radio. In this particular school—equivalent to a British
junior school—the children decided that they wanted to have
their own festival of arts, but didn't know enough about the
different art forms. First they collected news items about the
macro-festival from newspapers and took headings from them
like drama, opera, ballet, and started to make charts about each
one. As soon as anyone found out a new piece of information,
it was recorded in the relevant chart.

The teacher wrote on the chart the names of one or two well-
known exponents in each field and the children decided to write
to these people. Some of them were invited to the school and
accepted the invitation to come and tell the children more about
what a particular art form involved. All of the celebrities who
were written to gave some information, including one musician
who wrote back on manuscript paper! He was a trombonist
with a symphony orchestra and, as well as his letter and
pictures of the trombone which he sent, he gave the children the
addresses of other members of the orchestra who he thought
would be willing to co-operate. So the children wrote to
instrumentalists on the violin, French horn and timpani and
received letters from them too. The class eventually went to a
concert given by this orchestra, which had provided them with
so much information. When they returned to school they made

a plan to show not only the instruments and disposition of a symphony orchestra, which they had learned so much about, but also where their correspondents had their places in relation to the rest of the orchestra.

One of the actors whom the children wrote to gave details of how a radio programme he featured in was made. The programme chanced to be one of the class's favourites and they became very interested in the technical details. As part of their micro-festival, the children decided to make a 'radio programme' using his know-how, which they recorded on tape and then broadcast through the school's public address system.

20.2   The reading and writing activities involved in planning and putting on this festival of the arts all sprang from something which the children very much wanted to do and which was well suited to that group at that time. If the group you were teaching were neither interested nor gifted in music, drama, painting, or other arts, to channel them into producing such a festival would of course not provide relevance. But bearing this *caveat* in mind, are there any local festivals and traditions in your area which could be paralleled in your school? Events in the outside world, such as general elections, are often simulated in schools, but their outcome is a token; the newly elected 'Prime Minister' has no function when the day is done. But a festival involving arts, crafts, or entertainments is what it says it is and not just an exercise in role-play.

21

New Town—New Planners

21.1   Some children in an inner-city junior school were tired of their dreary environment and petitioned the staff to grow some trees in the yard. From this beginning an interest in their surroundings spiralled and gradually the whole school became involved in a plan to restructure the school yard completely. The children wrote to the local council, business firms, service clubs and anyone else they could think of for information, help and donations of trees and other amenities. The response was encouraging, so the children planned the total area of the school yard, allowing space for an adventure playground, trees, car parking and hard surface areas for ball games. They are now canvassing for further help from parents and other adults to achieve their vision.

21.2   When a town in Lanarkshire was designated Scotland's Sixth New Town, local feeling ran high about what the end result would be like. At the local primary school, a class of thirty-five nine- to ten-year-olds decided to undertake a project on the development of the New Town and began to discuss what was going to happen. The first session they had was spent talking about means of discovering information, as a result of which the children visited the local library. The librarian showed them how books were arranged on the shelves; half the class learned how the card index operated for fiction and non-fiction, while the other half worked with the encyclopaedias. The class returned to school with some difficult reading matter, including pamphlets from the Ministry of Labour. Obviously the 'reading age' of such documents was above the chronological age of these children but, with co-operative reading in groups of two or three, understanding grew and with it enthusiasm for the work. The class was divided into seven mixed-ability groups of five children, each allocated to one of the seven broad categories of question which the children had raised in their initial discussion: housing, jobs and industries, schools, roads, railways, parks and amenities.

The groups all got together to devise a questionnaire on the New Town, which they wrote and duplicated themselves and handed to their parents for completion. Each group was responsible for dealing with the returned answers which related to their special branch of the project. When the comments came in, the children read them, counted replies, drew graphs and wrote up a series of reports. The whole class collaborated on a letter which was sent to the Development Corporation for that area, requesting answers to specific questions. As a result, the Development Corporation invited the children to their head-quarters to put their questions directly to the New Town officials.

The visit stimulated even more interest as the children began more and more to relate their project work to the daily lives of the people in that area. They began to grasp some of the implications of the proposed development on their own home

area. When they visited the offices of the Development Corporation, they made notes on the answers to their questions and were
taken on a conducted tour of housing developments, industrial
areas and schools. They had collected more books and leaflets
on these visits, which they read in order to write up illustrated
reports for each group. All the reports were read and discussed
by all the other members of the class. To round off this stage,
the groups wrote thank-you letters to the Corporation officials,
saying what interested them most.

21.3   Next each special area group began an in-depth study.
The housing group decided to find out how a house was built.
They learned of the care involved in the preparation of plans
and what a long and important stage this was. As a result of this,
they learned a great deal about measurement which they passed
on to the rest of the class. After reading an advertising feature
on a new housing development, the group visited the building
site with a tape recorder and interviewed the contractor. Again,
verbal and written reports were prepared for the benefit of the
rest of the class. They also prepared a wall-chart which contained
job descriptions for work of an architect, plumber, plasterer and
joiner. Members of this group also wrote a short essay on
different types of houses and there was a discussion of a foundation report, accompanied by a foundation plan drawn to scale,
a description of the construction of walls and a description of the
roof and how it is put on to a house.

All these reports were accompanied by the appropriate
diagrams and a map showing the sources of the various building
materials. And all this was the work of one group! The other six
also prepared display material for others in the class to read.

21.4   The class then did some map work as a whole. After
their visit to the Development Corporation, when each child had
been given a map, their teacher discovered that they had all
spontaneously adopted the construction of an explanatory key
for the maps they had prepared in the group work. Now they
were given an aerial photograph of the town with contours
superimposed and asked to identify places they knew. They were
then given Ordnance Survey maps of the designated area and
asked to locate the same places. They worked from the
aerial photograph to the Ordnance Survey map and began to
understand more about the concept of maps and mapping. The
children then all drew their own plan of the New Town they

would like to see; their plans were circulated for class scrutiny and evaluation. The plan which was judged by the class to be best was of a new town called Avonhill, to be built beside the River Avon, and the children liked it so much that they constructed it in model form.

As the last stage of their project the children voted on whether they wanted a New Town at all and wrote their opinions on the proposals for their own town of Avonhill.

21.5 The teacher of this class found that the incentive to read and write about what was so closely related to their own lives led the children to tackle more difficult material than they would normally have read. Everything they wrote was read by other members of the class and ultimately by other members of the school and parents who became interested. Among the many positive aspects of the project was the team-work involved and the amount of research and involvement with the outside world that was needed.

Projects like this are not two a penny. There is no shortage of project work in schools, but many teachers have become disillusioned with it as a valuable educational technique. Fred Nind, for instance, head of the Coburg Junior School in Old Kent Road, London, believes that project work imposes artificial and often inappropriate limitations on the child's enquiries. Connections are strained, he says to try to make things fit in with the chosen 'theme', which is often imposed by the teacher. The teacher who monitored the New Town project was keen to develop literacy, but saw it in the context of many other skills like numeracy and map reading. She chose the project herself, but the reason that it developed as it did was that the children saw its relevance to their own lives and future. It is easy to be beguiled by the many possible ramifications that lead off from a project, and a teacher needs to ask the question 'So what?' before the children do.

But bearing this in mind, is there any work approaching the elaboration and sophistication of the New Town project which it would be appropriate to undertake with your junior or middle school pupils? Is the reading and writing involved strictly necessary for the progress of the work, or is it there just to create folders for display on parents' evenings? Can your children see the necessity of the reading and writing they are doing, or are they doing it to please you?

Part 3

Secondary School

22

A Better Place

22.1   Extending the context of organised projects, this is an account of work undertaken by pupils as part of a school's curriculum requirements. The topic of the survey was chosen by the girls themselves, who were a small group of sixteen-year-olds at what was then a grammar school in the Home Counties and is now a comprehensive. Having chosen their subject, which (like example 21) related to their own local community, another New Town, they planned and organised their survey themselves. At one end, they wrote a report on what they had done, which shows so clearly in their own words what skills they practised and discovered that it is worth printing substantial extracts from it.

22.2 ★ 'I don't want to pay £25,000, £10,000 or even £1,000 for growing geraniums in the middle of Marlowes', 'I'm sick of nicks and crannies in pavements which trip me up', 'We'd like a monorail in the town going from somewhere to somewhere', 'We'd like a boating lake in Gadebridge Park', . . . 'dustmen in uniform' . . . 'part-time school for little ones' . . . 'a university' . . .

These were just a few of the comments negative and positive that we received in connection with our survey on local amenities.

It is customary at our school, Apsley Grammar School, for all those who have finished their 'O' level exams at the end of June to take part in what is now known as the 'July Scheme'. We have a choice of activity for a period of two weeks, and a team of eight of us, all girls, wanted to do a social, consumer-orientated study. Our aim was to visit as many households as we could, with a view to finding out what people thought about their town, what they liked about it, and the ways in which it could be improved.

22.3   Preliminary stages

Early in the spring term we set up a small organising committee to deal with preparatory work so that we should be ready
to go out 'into the field' as soon as 'O' levels were over. How
were we going to find out what people thought? We decided
that the best way was to design a questionnaire that we our-
selves would complete as we interviewed people. (We rejected
the idea of postal questionnaires and of questionnaires distributed and called for later, because they were likely to produce
a poor return.) We thought too, that in view of the nearness of
the end of term, we ought to concentrate on an area close to
school, namely Bennetts End. We felt that this was fairly
representative of neighbourhood centres in general and that
it had a reasonable cross-section living in it. But what were
we to put in our questionnaires? In order to solve this
problem we drafted a letter, which the School Secretary
duplicated for us, and sent copies to about thirty eminent
local citizens asking for 'a brief but practicable statement on
how to improve this town'. We had fifteen replies to our letters, and it was on the basis of these that we then designed
our questionnaire relating to sports and leisure facilities for
younger children, facilities for the elderly, public transport,
traffic, roads, parking, local schools, shopping facilities,
housing and building programmes.

22.4   Secondary stage

Immediately after the exams we held a briefing session with
one of our teachers who has had consumer survey experience.
Our team also had to decide on sampling techniques: we
agreed on the simplest method—in view of the fact that a truly
random sample was not vital in this case—namely that of
interviewing every seventh householder in Bennetts End,
and a quick totting up of the number of houses in the area
suggested that we should get a final total of around two
hundred opinions. If we found that many women were out
during the daytime we would consider evening interviewing.
This was, in fact, not necessary. At this stage we had to decide
whether our first batch of questionnaires, now duplicated,
would actually 'work' on human beings, and so we did our
pilot run on willing members of staff and on parents living

near the school. Alterations were minimal. Now we learnt what it is like to have aching, swollen feet, because here we were out on our first stint of door-to-door interviewing. Electric bells don't always work properly, gate catches provide mysteries, little yapping dogs a persistent hazard. Some people open the door two inches wide and tell us to go away, others invite us in (we always work in pairs). Some people, elderly people or mothers with young children, saw in us a break from loneliness and so we went in and looked at scrapbooks and press-cuttings and photographs, and listened to tales of woe: one woman was very upset because the ceiling in her bedroom had fallen down for the second time and she kept on waiting and waiting for the plasterer to come back.

After a week of effort we have achieved two hundred interviews, covering the better part of Bennetts End. We decided to stop there as working out percentages would be so much easier!

22.5 What did we find out?

Firstly, we wanted some personal details but we decided not to ask possibly impertinent-sounding questions about age and occupation till the end when we had got people involved in our work. They wouldn't want to waste the information they had already given us by not completing the form! As it happened, no one appeared to resent our personal questions, and in the whole of our interviewing we had only one point-blank refusal, and that was from a woman who said, 'Well, I'm a bit thick, luv.'

(The children then added their analysis of the length of time people had lived in the town, of their age groups and of their occupations. They collated people's reasons for liking or disliking living in a new town, and their suggestions for improvement under the headings of sport, leisure entertainment, facilities for the elderly, public transport, roads and traffic, education, housing, shopping, medical and social welfare.)

22.6 What next?

We have spent two weeks of intensive work on this survey, not counting the background preparatory work which was done some time ago. The first week we spent on our house-to-house interviewing, the second on collation and writing up. We are well aware that Bennetts End, the second of the neighbourhood centres to be completed, is but part of our new town 'system', but we have no reason to suppose that the opinions put forward by Bennetts End householders are likely to be singularly different from those of the rest of the community in this area. (In any case, we did a quick spot check in Leverstock Green.) What have we achieved by our inquiry? We have caused people to reflect on the merits and demerits of the town in which they live; we have made them feel, even if only for a moment, that this is their town, that they can, by putting forward constructive suggestions, play a part in its future development. Scepticism about suggestions being ignored has been largely dispelled by the support we have received from the *Evening Echo* and the National Suggestions Centre, both of whom are willing to explore ideas. We think our role has been to bring about a link between our school and the community it serves. The community knows more about us and we know more about them.

Our next step must be not only to pick out obvious examples of public need (65 per cent begged for a Marks and Spencers), but also to take a look at all the ideas we have now catalogued, for the idea of one person may in itself be ultimately of more value than those for which there is a multiple 'vote'. In our case it is not necessarily the force of statistics that counts.

We must now seek to generate publicity for our report, to circulate it to people of local eminence who are likely to take note and act.

22.7   The girls working on this survey were intelligent GCE candidates and had thought carefully about what they were doing and how to do it. What is the role of the teacher in relation to a group and work of this kind? At what stages mentioned in the report might it have been appropriate for a teacher to make suggestions/offer expertise/guide work? In particular, what evaluation and development could have taken place? (There are some suggestions at the end of the report which could be extended.) Were there further opportunities for writing and reading of direct relevance to the topic which were not taken up? Is it possible in your school for pupils to type and duplicate materials such as questionnaires for themselves?

23

A Violent Beginning

23.1   The origin of these writing and reading activities was, to say the least, alarming. Four thirteen-year-old boys in an east London comprehensive had broken into an air-raid shelter which was being used as an emergency store for propane gas. The boys were truanting at the time and they began to smoke in the shelter; the explosion killed two of them and severely burnt the others, who were taken to hospital. One of the survivors was a member of a small remedial group in the school—reading age 8·6 years on the Holborn scale—and the remaining members of the group were very much affected by their friend's accident. They asked their teacher if they could carry out a project on safety.

23.2   On the first day of the project, the group went round the school buildings carrying clip-boards and noting any safety hazards. All six fire-buckets in the technical block were dis-covered to be empty, so the group returned to base and discussed what should be done. The correct procedure in the school was to report any such defect in writing to the deputy head. The group discussed the wording together and each boy wrote a rough draft of the note to be sent. They decided together on which was the best draft and the writer then made a fair copy which he took to the deputy head's In-tray. The group's teacher took the precaution of alerting her colleague to what was going on and he wrote a reply, addressed to the individual boy, and instituted appropriate action. The following week, when the group conducted another 'safety-round', they found all the fire-buckets brimful of sand. As their teacher remarked, 'very satisfying for the boys'.

23.3   Vigilance in the school was kept up and the group widened their activities to include writing to various agencies for specific information. They sent letters to the police, fire brigade, local authority, service and safety council, and other organisations, each boy writing at least two letters. Logs were kept of the letters written with their dates, authors and purposes. The boys next decided they needed some illustrative material, so took up photography. By making slides of local and school hazards such as busy zebra crossings, together with visits they had made to local fire and ambulance stations, the boys eventually created a film. They labelled each slide with its subject, frame number and the name of the boy who had taken it. Then the group discussed each slide, talking it through and making a tape recording. After listening to their recording again, they wrote down a commentary, which was typed for use as a script to their film. A new tape recording was made from this script, which was synchronised with the frames, to make a short film.

23.4   Each boy in the remedial group ended up with a file containing answers to letters he had written, notes on the use of the camera, notes for the film script and rough copies of letters to agencies and individuals. The group also had a log of photographs taken, together with an over-all post-book, logging letters sent and received. Members had also collected a great deal of display material, posters, booklets and so on, which all called for practice of reading skills. In making their film of safety hazards, they had to practise writing and indexing skills and the whole project had constantly called for planning and discussion at each stage. The physical outcome of the work formed the basis of a personal resource unit on safety which could be built up and added to over the years.

23.5   The stimulus for this project is of course, impossible to repeat or simulate. Yet one can imagine that the idea of finding out about safety precautions and regulations might have been unappealing and boring to a group of thirteen-year-olds if it had not been for their close involvement with such a horrific experience. In this instance, as often in others (see examples 5.2, 15, 16, 17, 24, 25 and 26), writing and reading activities provided a means of doing something positive about anxiety and fear. The teacher was not only encouraging literacy in a backward group, but was contributing to their personal growth by helping them to cope with their natural emotional reaction to the death and injury of their peers. It brings us back again to the need for teachers to know their pupils as individuals, what their hopes and fears and interests are; you can't be relevant in a vacuum.

23.6 This particular project might have been developed to cover more aspects of school safety, if the children would have remained interested and engaged enough. They had already surveyed the buildings for hazards in general, but might have divided them into the points of view of (a) pupils, (b) teachers, (c) other staff, (d) parents and (e) other visitors. In surveying buildings, there is a lot to be learnt about standards, materials and maintenance which is very relevant to adult life. The Health Education Council puts out leaflets on safety in the home, showing danger spots and death traps for everyone, with special reference to young children and old people. It might be useful to introduce such literature to a class that had shown particular concern about safety. What further reading, writing and planning activities might have been relevant to this group, or to any other group interested in personal and public safety?

24
Underground Activities

24.1 The following remarkable project was undertaken by pupils at a special school for physically handicapped children in north London. The nature of their handicaps was tremendously varied, but all the children were taken to and from school in special buses throughout their school years. Some of the pupils in their last year had begun to worry about how to cope with travelling around London; it became a matter of some urgency as they contemplated what jobs they would be able to apply for and how they were to manage journeys to and from work. There was no regulation to prevent them making school journeys by public transport if school and parents were willing, but in practice this was never done. In the course of a social studies class of school-leavers, it emerged in discussion on transport that some members of the group had never travelled on the London Underground. The teacher toyed with the idea of taking individuals to travel on the tube in order to lessen their anxiety, but so many worries had been revealed by the discussion that they decided to organise a group project.

24.2   Their aim was to find out how accessible the London
Underground system was to physically handicapped people.
If the project proved feasible, they intended to keep the
information for use in school for future pupils who were about
to leave. Before the children started, their teacher visited London
Transport officials at a main line station and met their legal
representative. She discovered from them that there was no
document already in existence which was equivalent to the one
her pupils were planning to compile. In addition she was
informed that only one station had a ramp and that very few
stations now had lifts; this meant that the pupils would not be
able to take wheel-chairs. There was only one member of the
group who was dependent on a chair, so he was given the task
of processing material already supplied by London Transport.
Most of the information received had been organised on the
basis of the different Underground lines. The boy in the wheel-
chair began to re-organise this into alphabetical order of
stations.

The rest of the group chose a sample of the stations to check
accessibility factors such as levels, ramps, escalators, lifts; they
chose to check different facilities on each line. They would set
off from the Underground station nearest to the school and travel
to their chosen destination, where they were sometimes met and
escorted by a station official. For each visit, a group leader
volunteered to get the rest of the class to their destination. In
order to make this route-planning and travelling as near to adult
experience as possible, the group's teacher had asked station
officials not to say anything if they went in the wrong direction
or made a mistake at an interchange of lines. It was the job of that
day's leader to make sure that they all took the correct route and
adjust any mistakes made in the course of the journey. Each
visit was preceded by a class discussion using a tube map, so that
routes and changes were planned beforehand and all the children, as well as the day's leader, were given practice in map-
reading and diagrammatic conventions.

Time was the greatest problem for this handicapped group,
as they had to work within the school curriculum. They had no
mishaps or accidents, although contingency plans had been
made for delay through epilepsy. Several children had walking
aids of some kind and many of these had not used the Underground before. The children did not conduct their survey during
rush-hours, but the confidence they gained in travelling was

more likely to help them when eventually faced with a more crowded situation.

24.3 When the project was completed to their satisfaction the children wrote, co-operatively, their own *Guide to London's Underground* for the physically handicapped. In writing the guide, the children became even more enthusiastic about what they were doing and wondered whether, as well as helping future pupils in their school, it might be of use to other handicapped members of the community. It did not take long for them to decide that they would like their guide to be published. As a part of their work they had written to London Transport, who had been co-operative with the whole project, to the Special School Inspectors and to various handicapped public figures, such as the late Michael Flanders, and had become more used to making their opinions publicly heard. Before long the Central Council for the Disabled had agreed to publish the children's guide and it is still available from them (at the time of going to press) as the only document of its kind. The children were disappointed with the end product, however, because the print was so tiny, and they felt that handicapped people, who often suffer from more than one disability, would find it physically very hard to read. They wrote to the Central Council expressing their reactions to the publication. In spite of these production defects, the report received quite a bit of publicity in the press and on the radio, which was very rewarding for the children involved. They received letters from people who had heard of what they were doing, but the greatest satisfaction for them had been in following a project through from its conception and planning to its completion.

24.4 The compiling of the *Guide* involved this group of school leavers in many reading and writing activities. They wrote and received letters, planned routes with the use of the tube maps, compiled lists of stations and their facilities. In their field work they had to read signs, notices, maps and instructions for automatic barriers and ticket machines. They had the help of London Transport officials and visited a London Transport training centre at White City. Their motivation throughout was to be able to use London's busiest and most far-reaching transport system, which was for them the key to developing normal careers and social lives.

Their teacher was one of the few I have talked to who had

thought seriously about how the project could develop and what modifications could be made to it. She plans to up-date the report with another group of school leavers, with the double purpose of checking on how facilities have changed and of giving a new group the confidence to use the system. She says: 'I do not know whether the children use the handbook, but they do use the Underground. In fact on a school visit shortly after this, to an art gallery, they suggested we went by Underground and not school bus and that we took somebody in a wheel-chair. Before this survey, this suggestion would not have been made.'

It is another example of drawing on a group's worries about the future when they are about to leave school. This was a group with obvious specific reasons for being nervous about travel and normal functioning within the community, but anyone about to leave the security of a system in which he or she has spent at least eleven years is bound to have some doubts and fears. What can be done to help your school leavers cope with their adult lives?

25

Yvonne's Spots

25.1   The project which follows evolved out of a situation very relevant to secondary school pupils. The children were a mixed low-ability fourth year social studies group, with a reputation for being difficult. Nevertheless, they conducted the following ambitious investigation into shampoos, the results of which were welded into a survey report and typed out in a commerce period by five girls rather more enthusiastic than the rest. The original stimulus was a spontaneous pre-lesson comment by Yvonne who had just been to the doctor about her acne: 'He says I got to get me hair cut, and wash it more so's not to get spots.' How often did people wash their hair? What did they wash it with? Was what manufacturers said about grease and split ends true? Here are the results of the children's investigations; the comments remain as originally written, but the background information has had the spellings corrected and any necessary punctuation added. In essence it remains their work, related to their interests.

25.2 ★ Taking a look at shampoos

'They would be better for washing dog': did we all agree with this comment from Peter on modern shampoos? Our following report will show the opinions of the remainder of our year group.

Why we undertook our inquiry

During a discussion on advertising some of us mentioned that we didn't think that shampoos always did what they were supposed to do—all this on television about making hair glossy, nourishing it and mending split ends. At this point the *Which?* report (February 1973) came out and some of us who are keen on cosmetics and hair read bits of this and began to wonder if spending money on shampoos wasn't just pouring it down the drain. And the *Sunday Times*, in an article on hair care, hinted that you might do just as well using *Teepol*, which is a sort of washing-up liquid made by Shell. We were glad when Miss got some free samples of *Silvikrin Lemon and Lime* and *Alpine Herb* shampoo, so that we could not only make inquiries about people's personal practices, but so that we could actually try out an actual product for nothing.

We made up a list of questions and gave a copy to all the pupils in our fourth year social studies group, even to the boys—and not one of them protested or said he didn't wash his hair. Our questions were divided into three parts.

(*a*) personal details and problems, and people's attitude to shampoos in general.
(*b*) facts and opinions about the samples of shampoo which we then distributed.
(*c*) opinions on the results of hair washing using these shampoos.

We completed (*a*) and (*b*) at school, but (*c*) obviously had to be done at home. We numbered our question-sheets so that we could check on people who might want to lose them, and also so that we would know where we were when it came to writing up the results.

There were twenty-eight girls and twelve boys in our group,

and they all gave back our questions on time. Ten of us volunteered to work out the results as part of a CSE project.

25.3   How would you describe your hair?

twenty people had greasy hair
sixteen had normal hair
three had dry hair

About half the class said they had real problems: 'I have flaky white bits falling out of my hair especially when it starts to itch, and you scratch it'; or 'My hair is more greasy than most people', or 'The doctor says it causes my spots. I've got dandruff', 'I get a lot of split ends, it goes all frizzy as well'.

nine people had dandruff
five had split ends
five suffered from electricity
two had frizz
twenty-two didn't know if they had problems (so presumably they didn't)

We found that people got very troubled about their problems and embarrassed about their appearance, but they didn't know who to go to for advice—except perhaps their doctor, and doctors tend to say lots of floppy greasy hair hanging down over your face, or flakes of dandruff dropping around, make your spots worse. It doesn't help much to be told that it is a problem of our age group and that we will grow out of it. It's now that looking nice matters.

How often do you wash your hair?

nine washed it every two to three days
nineteen washed it every four to five days
twelve washed it once a week

This was, of course, what people *said* they did. Nobody would want to admit to not having washed his or her hair for a month. Perhaps we ought to have asked the question another way: 'When did you last wash your hair?' and worked from there. Nevertheless, we guess that those with grease and dandruff would wash their hair pretty often.

Which shampoo do you usually use?

nine people bought a shampoo to stop grease
six bought one to make their hair shiny
six used whatever their mum bought
four bought a shampoo for dandruff
four bought one to mend split ends

and the remainder bought any shampoo that happened to take their fancy at that moment.

The most popular brand used in the group was *Sunsilk* with ten votes—no other shampoo approached this in popularity, though a further ten people used different kinds of medical shampoos like *Tegrin* and *Clinic*.

Are there any shampoos you have tried and won't use again?

eleven people didn't like *Protein 21*
three didn't like *Loxene*
two didn't like *Palmolive*
two didn't like *Tegrin*

Fifteen out of our group of forty had found a shampoo they would never use again. (Our numbers add up to more than fifteen because some people didn't like more than one brand.) *Protein 21*—'It just doesn't work', 'Becos it make my head itch', 'I ment to stop split end but it don't', 'It leaves your hair in knots', 'It makes your hair more greasy'.
Medical shampoos—'It smell vile and give me dandruff worse', 'Medicated ones don't lather well and don't do any more good'.

Do you buy shampoos in small packs or large sizes?

twenty-six always bought large sizes ('It's cheap', 'So we don't run out')
nine bought small sizes ('I use too much from a bottle')
five bought some of each 'If I'm trying a new shampoo I buy a small pack, if I like it my mum buy a big pack', 'If you don't like it it's not a wasted bottle')

Do you use shampoo only?

fifteen used shampoo only
seventeen used shampoo and conditioner together
six used shampoo and then conditioner separately
two didn't answer

The seventeen people using the mixture liked to buy their shampoo that way because 'It's more convenient', or because 'I couldn't be bothered to put in a different conditioner'.

The fifteen using just a shampoo did so because 'I like it that way', 'I like it just sompoo', because 'Others are expensive'.

The six using shampoo and then a separate conditioner did so because 'I get a shine and healthy look'.

Where is this particular shampoo made?

Everyone except Gary found out from looking at the sachet carefully that the shampoo was made in 'Silvikin Laboraties'.

Are the ingredients clearly listed?

Most people didn't know what our question meant and either left the answer blank or wrote down '*Alpine Herb*' or '*Lemon and Lime*'; but three people—and these were the correct ones—said they couldn't find out anywhere exactly what went into this shampoo, and it might matter if you had an 'adlergy'.

Do you like the pack?

twenty-five people liked the pack 'It's small and can put in a pocked can be folded to', 'You can fold it sqce it and it won't break', 'It pritty and the colores go well together'.
five didn't like it much 'It is uninteresting and doesn't draw your attention'.
ten were indifferent 'I suppose it's O.K.'

Make a list of words you don't understand:

Alpine Herb: four people didn't know what this meant in spite of the picture on the front.

Organic: twenty-four people had no idea what this meant, and the twenty-fifth said it reminded him of an advertisement about manure.

Nutrient: twelve people had no idea what this meant.

Formulated: five didn't know this one.

Conditioning: six said they didn't understand this one either, which made us wonder how they were able to answer the question about shampoos and conditioners in general!

Lankness and Excessive: three people found each of these words difficult.

In general, our group thought it would be much better if details about the shampoo were written in simpler words that everyone could understand, especially as they got a bit suspicious about long, scientific words.

How did you open the pack?

Thirty-one people thought this was rather a silly question as there are instructions on the sachet about cutting the corner with scissors ('I cut where it says cut here')
seven people nevertheless opened it with their teeth ('With my teef')
two tore open the packet ('I ripped open the top' or 'I tear the packet').
So, nine out of forty did not carry out instructions properly (perhaps because they didn't have scissors handy), but even so didn't find any real difficulty.

Was there enough shampoo?

twenty-two people thought there was enough
twelve said too much
four said not enough
two didn't answer

What did you think about its scent?

Most people liked the scents of both kinds of shampoo—'a nice smell', 'clean and strong', 'It's a pity it didn't last longer'. There were ten people who just said 'It's O.K.', but two thought that *Alpine Herb* was 'perpery' and 'It's a bit horrible but that doesn't matter as it soon wore off'.

What did you think about its colour and texture?

Jane's was the most sensible remark because she said, 'The couler is not important of the texture its how it works that counts'. Thirty people used words like 'fluffy', 'soft', 'smooth', 'all geley'. Ten were less impressed and thought it 'waterey', 'it could've been thicker', 'runney', or 'slimey'.

The final result, would you buy it again?

twenty-seven said they would not buy it again.
eleven said they would, including one who was going straight out to buy a family size bottle.
two didn't know.

25.4   This group of ROSLA pupils were enthusiastic about tackling in school something which was related to their 'real' life outside. The same group had done a smaller project on shoes after one boy had proudly displayed new platform soles weighing 5 pounds and had been interested enough to make charts, budget forms and questionnaires and collect background information. The result of that project was that those teenagers made inquiries before buying shoes and knew what to do if they proved unsatisfactory. Projects of this kind which involve pupils in relevant reading and writing are forming a bridge between school and adult life, when decision-making passes more prominently into the hands of the individual. What other appropriate topics involving reading, writing and planning could be used to help ROSLA year pupils cope with the transition?

26

After the Flood

26.1   On a day in August 1975, when all the rest of London and most of the British Isles was enjoying fine weather, a thunderstorm gathered over Hampstead Heath and released enough rain to cause severe flood damage to an area of only a few square miles. This freak storm created emergency conditions for hundreds of local residents, rendering homes uninhabitable, ruining possessions and causing water pipes to overflow and cause further damage. When the children of Hampstead Comprehensive went back to school in September, most had seen some of the worst results of the flood six weeks before and some had been directly affected in their own homes. A group of fifteen-year-olds doing community studies wanted to follow up the effects of the flooding on the local community and to see if they could give any positive help. As preliminary to their main survey, they made contact with the local community centre in West Hampstead which recommended three people it thought would be willing to talk to the children about their experiences.

Initially, the children took tape recorders and went to interview the three people suggested by the centre. They talked through their experiences and reactions on the night when their homes had so suddenly filled with water. On returning to school the children played through the tapes and discussed what the major points were to be dealt with. From this discussion they made the first draft of a questionnaire which they planned to take out to residents in the most badly affected local roads. The children contacted a local councillor who came to talk to the group; in the light of his experience of residents' complaints and needs, he suggested modifications which were incorporated into the final questionnaire.

26.2   Questionnaire:

Hampstead School Flood Survey

Name: . . . .

Address: . . . .

1 How long have you lived here? . . . . years.
2 How were you affected by the floods?
   Very badly . . . . . . badly . . . . . . fairly . . . . . . slightly. . . . . .
   not at all . . . . . .
3 How much damage was done to your property? £. . . . .
4 What injuries, if any, were suffered? . . . .

5 (a) Did you get any help? From the council ....
                            From D.H.S.S. ....
                            From neighbours ....
  (b) What sort of help was it? ....
  ....
  (c) How quickly did help come? Fast .... Medium ....
      Slow ...... Too late ...... Not at all ....
6 After the flood could you still sleep here? Yes/No.
7 (a) If no, were you offered temporary accommodation? ....
      By Camden Council ...... Voluntary body ....
      Friends ....
  (b) How long did you have to stay away? ....
8 Is your home still damp? Yes/No.
9 Is there a smell? (What sort?) Yes/No.
10 Has all the rubbish been removed? Yes/No.
11 What help if any do you need now from public services? ....
   ....
12 How quickly were gas and electricity repairs completed?
   Fast ...... Medium ...... Slow ...... Not at all ......
13 (a) Thinking back did you know where to get help? Yes/No.
   (b) If yes, where from? ....
14 Do you know that you can apply for a grant or loan from
   D.H.S.S. towards covering your loss? Yes/No.
15 (a) Do you think that the Council has fulfilled its responsi-
       bilities adequately? Yes/No.
   (b) If no, what further should have been done? ....
16 What suggestions do you have to prevent the recurrence of
   such a disaster? ....

26.3   When the questionnaire had been typed and duplicated,
the children took it round to three local roads which had been
badly flooded and two slightly farther away, one of which had
its own neighbourhood action committee on the damage. In
the end, fifty questionnaires were completed, which was fewer
than the children had hoped, but enough to draw some conclusions from. When the questionnaires had all been returned, the
group arranged for a Camden councillor to attend a meeting at
the Community Centre and wrote letters to all the people they
had interviewed inviting them to attend the meeting. They
then wrote up a report on the results of the survey. This was
done co-operatively, but their teacher adjusted spelling and
grammar before it was typed and duplicated.

★ Results of Hampstead School Flood Survey

Fifty homes were visited in Sumatra Road, Dennington Park Road, Pandora Road, Greencroft Gardens and Goldhurst Terrace.

The major points revealed by this survey were as follows:

Pandora, Dennington Park, and Sumatra Road

There had been extensive damage—the bill for repairs in ten badly hit homes amounted together to over £15,000.

Few people had known where to turn for help.

They were grateful for Council help when it came, but many now feel that it was inadequate.

60% of those interviewed did not know about the grants or loans from the D.H.S.S.

80% of the homes were still smelly and damp.

Particular requests to the council were for larger sewers and more efficient relief services for flooded areas.

Goldhurst Terrace

Again extensive damage had occurred and many persons said they were in need of financial assistance, but 90% did not know about the grants or loans from D.H.S.S.

The Council had acted promptly to bring in electric dryers, but had been slow to remove rubbish and unblock drains. All the homes visited were still affected by damp. Requests to the council were for larger sewers and better maintenance of drains.

Greencroft Gardens

Damage reported was far less extensive, but help from the Council seems to have been poor. Dryers were not readily available and rubbish had to be cleared by the residents. All those interviewed requested the Council to provide larger and better maintained drains.

26.4 The children next collaborated on a letter to the Mayor about their findings. On the surface, this seemed an excellent project, closely related to the children's own lives, taking them out into the community, preparing them for adult decisions and responsibilities and involving reading and writing in the work undertaken. But when I spoke to the teacher concerned, he seemed disappointed with the outcome and felt that the children had also been rather disillusioned. They had hoped to complete far more than fifty questionnaires and they got very little response for the meeting that they arranged with the councillor. Little evaluation seems to have taken place about how the activities could have been better managed or whether they were the most appropriate ones in the circumstances. It was a case where action had to be taken fairly quickly while residents were still sufficiently in touch with the events of six weeks earlier to be willing to participate. Nevertheless, there had been extensive planning, so it is worth considering why the result was unsatisfactory to teacher and pupils. They might have asked themselves the following questions:

26.5   Do you think, in the light of the time that had elapsed since the flood, that the survey was the most useful kind of action to undertake? If not, what else would have been more appropriate? The meeting with the councillor was held in the middle of the day and very few residents turned up. Could it have been held at any other time? Is there any provision in the syllabus for activities to be carried on out of school hours and still to count as part of project time? If not, is it ever worth organising something as a part of school hours which needs the attendance and co-operation of people who are at work? If the flood, or any other emergency, had taken place in term-time, how easy would it have been to capitalise on an event of such local and personal interest and disrupt the existing syllabus? Was enough of the writing, reading and planning in the hands of the children? Were they encouraged to ask of themselves what they would do differently if conducting such a survey again, in the light of their experience?

27

Writing for a Change

27.1   This project originated with teachers, but became very much the pupils' own work, related to their own goals and absorbing their interest. It arose out of discussions between a teachers' first form planning group at a secondary school and members of the staff of the Schools Curriculum Project at Queen's University in Belfast. They were concerned about the inadequacy of the induction procedures for children moving from primary to secondary schools and felt that the secondary school teachers hadn't enough time available to improve the situation. The teachers at this secondary school decided to ask fourth form ROSLA pupils if they would be willing to help in an experiment to ease the transition period for younger pupils. It was decided to ask the ROSLA girls because they had no pressing examination commitments and would be returning to school for another year and could follow up their work with the primary school leavers who would by then be first formers.

27.2   This request for help struck an immediate chord with the fourth years and many more volunteered for the experiment than the twenty who were chosen. They first attended a short course organised by the project staff in the local teacher's centre, at which the reasons for the experiment were explained and the students then split into groups to discuss their perception of the needs of primary school children. The girls clearly recalled their own excitement and anxiety when they had started at the secondary school and were very keen to help. They themselves suggested keeping accounts of their visits to primary schools, some of which are quoted below. Arrangements were made for each girl to visit a contributory primary school for half a day each week for six weeks, usually during less formal work periods, in order to be able to talk to the children more freely. They agreed to meet again for an evaluation session before they finished their visits.

27.3 The fourth formers kept diaries of their visits in which they recorded not only the primary children's worries and expectations but their own reactions and what they were learning in the course of the project. Quite often, when the primary children got to know them better, the fourth formers were asked to help them with their work.

★ I took a group and my friend took a group and we helped them with their reading and if they didn't know a word or understant it we would try and explain it to them. They are very friendly and you can get on with them all, allright.

The next week we gave them reading one book one at a time and helped them with it and then we had another talk with them and answered their question. But I look forward to going to the schools each week and helping the girls with their problems and answering their questions as well as helping them with their lessons which I enjoy.

One girl systematically collected and listed the fears about secondary school which the primary children had:

1 They are afraid of breaking the rules
2 being late on the first day
3 not knowing wear the classroom is that they will have to go to
4 not having the right uniform
5 not being able to do the work
6 being bullied
7 afraid of the teachers
8 afraid of being slaped
9 afraid of getting into trouble
10 afraid of the teacher's picking on them all the time

The secondary students were often surprised at the quality of the work being done in the primary schools they visited and learned something themselves from the lessons they attended, like this one on Nature: 'It was very interesting and we as well as the girls learnt a great deal.' It was also an eye-opener for the fourth formers to see how the primary school regarded them. As one girl remarked, 'as they watched us come along the path you would have swore we were from space the way they jumped up to the windows and shouted Miss here they come.'

The same girl wrote the following extracts:

★ At the end of the evening I felt I had achifed something and that the girls knew more about secondary schools.

★ The kind of questions they ask. Will we have any of our friends in the same class as us? Do you get lots of book and plenty of homework? What are the teachers like are they wicket?

★ While I sat with a group of girls they all looked forward to leaving primary school because they could then join youth clubs and act older and get into over 12's disco's.

★ One thing they are looking forward too and that is getting a master for subjects which they have never had.

★ To hear some of them talk you think the school had hundreds of coridoors and before they even get to the school they wanted to know what subjects they would get in second year.

27.4   It was from comments and observations like these, together with interviews of children already in their first year at secondary school that staff and pupils compiled the booklet *Changing Schools*. It is an attempt to help parents help their children by letting them both know what life is like in secondary school and how it differs from the primary school. *Changing Schools* is only the first of a series of booklets planned to be given to parents to keep them in touch with different aspects of their children's life at the new school.

27.5   Spontaneously, when the visits were over, the girls asked if they could help the teachers with first form classes when the new pupils started next term. Arrangements were made to use them as auxiliaries for a few periods each week in integrated studies (History, Geography and English in this school). One first form teacher set aside some time to take the senior girls for a lesson each week in which they go through the curriculum material to be used with the first form. These materials involve a variety of reading skills and the teachers say that the ROSLA girls have gained a lot from reading with the purpose of needing to teach from the materials and then implementing what they had understood in the classroom. The girls have proved particularly helpful working with small groups and with individual children who have reading diffi-culties. One girl from another school in the same area who became involved in a similar project went on to investigate the possibilities of teacher-training.

27.6   These activities, although not stemming from the pupils' own suggestions, were highly motivating. The fourth formers were sufficiently close in age to the potential first formers to remember their own experiences and were able to pass on their own recipes for coping far better than any teacher. They became increasingly more articulate as they wrote their diaries and needed to find expression for the complex states of mind they discovered in the children; the reports were then used and read by themselves and others to make a valuable document for parents and children. An added bonus was the way in which they became involved with helping younger children in their reading. But perhaps most important and most purposeful for them was the way in which they were able, at a time when they had only a year to go before their own transition into a world whose rules they were unsure of and whose punishment and reward system they feared, to help other children in a similar situation which they had already coped with in the past. What are the relations between primary and secondary schools in your area? Could some useful and relevant reading and writing be done by school leavers in your secondary school to bridge the gap? Is there any local equivalent to the *Changing Schools* booklet produced in Belfast? If not, can your seniors research and produce one?

28

Something to Remember

28.1   This project, far from originating with the pupils concerned, grew out of their reluctance and distaste, but gradually involved them as deeply in functional reading and writing as any other I have mentioned. Five 'difficult' girls whose reading skills were not good and who had never written much, researched, wrote, typed and duplicated a booklet for foreign exchange visitors to their school. *Souvenir '74* began when this group expressed their bias against the visitors and grew out of the teacher's suggestion that life in a new country might be difficult and confusing for the visitors. What follows is taken from the teacher's report of the book's production.

28.2 Introducing critical awareness

Children are used to being passively exposed to facts at home, at school, at work and in the media: here, in the creation of their book, these girls saw information in a new light. For in this new activity of theirs, it was their responsibility to be the providers of facts, finding out where to go, where to look, whom to ask. They had to collect, select, evaluate, verify, to doubt the words and writing of others until scrupulous checking could provide confirmation. (They learned the hard way here, having made a mistake over postal rates to France and then having to stick typed 'erratum' slips in their books. 'Why can't we just say "mistake", Miss?') And always they had to approach their work with an unswerving attitude of critical awareness.

They began to appreciate that they could collect and compare prices of tea bags (a good present for *Grand'mère*, they thought) or tights (for an older sister), but no personal preferences; for people are likely to vary in their reaction to taste, smell, sound, colour and texture. In their evaluation of souvenirs available in their town they became aware of this force of preference divorced from reason: they instinctively favoured a vulgar little pot boy called Wee Weepy Willie which you filled with water and then awaited obvious results. But in their growing maturity they realised that at the same price a discreet Melamine ashtray dish of St George and his dragon was likely to be a better buy for unknown foreigners with unascertainable tastes.

28.3 Breaking down the subject barriers

Though this particular project was carried out within the broad framework of Social Studies, it included English in the writing-up, Maths and European Studies in its price comparisons and tabulations of British and European sizes, weights and measures, Environmental Studies and Geography in its appreciation of leisure facilities available, Home Economics in the wide shopping content, Law, Current Affairs, Commerce and Business Studies. And it provided real work experience as they typed, learned to use Letraset headings and illustrations, prepared their manuscript ready for offset litho at the local Teachers' Centre.

28.4   Achieving relevance within the curriculum

The girls were not, in their British insularity, exactly predisposed towards foreigners at first (though they did end up by wanting to take a party out on a shopping expedition). Nevertheless, they could see a very real point in producing their little book. It wasn't just another exercise: it was something where the end-product was actually going to be used. And in its variety it was never boring; the changing tasks and demands for different skills providing a continuing motivating force.

28.5   Providing out-of-school opportunities

The project gave the girls the chance to get out of the classroom, and in doing this to achieve responses and relationships more easily, not only within the peer group but also with Miss. In their earliest preparatory surveys on telephone systems, the aims of some at least had seemed to get rid of Miss, nip round the corner for a smoke, and try to get home early. But these evasions soon stopped, so did the smoking, and a proper team relationship was established.

28.6   The pay-off for these girls was the booklet itself and watching the French children use it when they came to the school. One page of *Souvenir '74* gives the flavour of the project:

★USEFUL FACTS TO KNOW ABOUT THE BRITISH

1 They eat with a knife in their right hand and a fork in their left.
2 Milk is brought to the house by the milkman every day, in pints.
3 People are usually very orderly and queue for things like buses.
4 They stand on the right going down escalators in the underground.
5 They don't think greeting people (shaking their hand and kissing them on both cheeks) is so very important.
6 They love listening to weather forecasts on the radio and TV. Most people still work in Fahrenheit and not Centigrade.
7 They are always eating sweets—more each week than anybody else in the world.

8 They eat bread at breakfast time and at tea time, usually with butter, but not at lunch or dinner time.
9 They don't tip the girl who shows them to their seat in the cinema.
10 Motorists usually respect people's rights on pedestrian crossings. You have to watch out more in London, though.

FOOD TO TRY: HAVE YOU TASTED . . . ?

1 Fish and chips
2 Shepherd's pie
3 Fruit jelly
4 Sausages and mash
5 Apple tart
6 Steak and kidney pie
7 Trifle
8 Steamed sponge pudding
9 Macaroni cheese
10 An English breakfast

28.7 As an example of involving children through their dislikes and prejudices rather than their preferences, *Souvenir '74* is a rare success. Such an approach obviously needs sensitive handling by the teacher and a constant awareness of what negative feelings can be helped through the project. As soon as

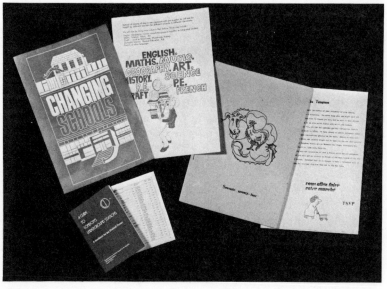

these xenophobic girls put themselves into the position of aliens in a foreign land, they found their undertaking full of interesting and rewarding avenues of exploration. Until they had done that, they regarded the expected visitors as intruders to be resented and would never have considered doing anything to make their stay easier or more pleasant.

As their teacher demonstrated, they acquired and practised many skills in writing the booklet which may be of use in their adult working lives. They soon developed the desire to do everything by themselves and make the production their own.

If your children were to prepare a booklet for foreign visitors, what would you expect the list of contents to look like? What would the index, if it had one, look like? Can you think of other situations in which relevant reading and writing activities could be the means of exploring and resolving negative feelings?

29

What Are You Going To Do About It?

29.1   It was a small group of indignant fifteen-year-olds who originated the next series of reading and writing activities. The girls had complained that it wasn't fair that shopkeepers were being asked to vote whether shops should continue to keep their traditional halfday closing or to be open for six days each week, when shoppers were being given no say in the matter. After lively discussion, their teacher put the ball firmly in their court by asking, 'What are you going to do about it?' Their answer is contained in the following survey.

29.2 ★ Six-day shopping in Hemel Hempstead

'I am glad somebody has taken the trouble to ask us what we think', 'It's a one-sided view if you only get the view of shopkeepers', 'Shoppers get pushed around too much; after all, we pay for a service.'

Hemel Hempstead Borough Council is at present asking shopkeepers in the centre of the town to vote whether they are in favour of being open six days a week. At the moment there is an Act of Parliament which makes most shops close for half a day during the working week. If this law is to be changed, there must be a ballot of shopkeepers. This is what is happening now: the Council has sent round a questionnaire, to be completed by April 17th, to which shopkeepers must answer 'yes' or 'no'. Unfortunately, the words are difficult to understand, and there have already been complaints about 'legal language' published in the *Evening Echo*; we too found the question hard to understand:

'Are you in favour of the Borough Council making an order to exclude all shops in the High Street/Marlowes area of the Borough from the provision of the Shops Act 1950 which requires shops (unless excluded by other provisions) to be closed for the serving of customers not later than one o'clock in the afternoon on one week day in every week?'

So far, no one has set about asking shoppers what they want or need in respect of shop-opening hours—and the quotations at the beginning of this report show their reactions to our survey. We decided to find out what shoppers think as part of our CSE Social Studies work, using a very simple questionnaire.

29.3 What we did

A team of six of us went into the centre of Hemel Hempstead in mid-afternoon on a fine, sunny day in early April when there were plenty of people rather leisurely strolling about and not minding much about being stopped. We were very worried at first at the idea of approaching people even though we had practised muttering to each other, 'I am a pupil at Longdean School and would like to know what you think about shopping in Hemel Hempstead. Would you mind answering a very few quick questions?' Tina knew she would blush scarlet. Shirley wondered what she would do if someone was rude to her. Lorraine thought she wouldn't be able to write down the answers fast enough. But after the first few times, we felt much better and Anne even began to enjoy herself. We didn't work on a quota sample basis, which means that you ask particular numbers of people between 16–24, others between 25–34, others between 35–44, others 45–65,

and a final group over 66; for one thing, we didn't want to
ask people their ages, and we didn't think we would be good at
guessing accurately. But we did take care to balance out the
people we interviewed, getting a selection of young people,
of mothers with young babies and toddlers, of older women,
pensioners, of men—though two-thirds of the people we
talked to were women. We included a blind man with a white
stick to see if he had special problems. During our afternoon's
work, with a coffee break in the middle when we compared
notes and chatted to an old lady who did so wish for 'a nice
little tea shop in Marlowes that didn't smell of fish and chips',
we interviewed 100 people. Actually, the hundredth was Mrs
Brown the Senior Mistress who not only answered our
questions but asked us a new set of her own! It is the views
of these people that we classify below:

number of people wanting six-day opening	42%
number of people not wanting six-day opening	43%
number not knowing or not caring	15%
Total	100%

The conclusion from these figures, on the basis of our
admittedly experimental survey, can only be that which ever
way the shopkeepers decide to vote they will have both
support and opposition from the public. We were a bit
worried by the number of people who, instead of saying, 'I
don't know' answered with a shrug of their shoulders, 'I
couldn't care less.' There must be some reason for this kind
of answer.

29.4   Why did the people who answered 'yes' want shops open for six days?

39 people (out of the 42 who responded) gave reasons:
21 thought it would be more convenient being able to shop
   whenever they wanted from Monday through to Saturday,
   and eight among them said that longer hours would be
   particularly useful to them as working women.
13 thought that half-day systems were 'muddling', 'confusing' or 'uncertain' especially if you came into Hemel
   Hempstead from somewhere like Stanmore.
 3 people reminded us that it is a shop's job to serve and
   be open to fulfil the customer's needs.

Though we didn't ask a specific question, some of the 43 people who didn't feel in favour of six-day trading insisted on giving their reasons.

12 felt that it was 'not necessary' either for them personally or for people generally. Three of these even went so far as to say that people ought to learn to plan their time properly and use such shopping 'space' there already was.

4 thought that shopkeepers were having a hard time and didn't want to impose on them

2 didn't want anything further to happen to push small shops out of business

2 felt that longer opening could be unfair to shop assistants.

29.5   Which particular shops did people want open?

Some people mentioned shops by name, others by category. Though there were small groups of people wanting Boots and Woolworths open, or less specifically clothes shops, electricians, car accessory shops, the biggest response came from those who wanted food shops open: 13 wanted longer hours for food shops, together with a further four who wanted Sainsbury's open.

Even those who didn't want six-day trading sometimes put in a plea for bakers to be open every day 'since bread doesn't keep now as it used to do'.

Which places—other than shops—did people want open?

These comments are particularly important since we didn't ask any questions about them. If people raise such matters without prompting, then they are likely to be of significance:

4 people wanted the public library open on Wednesday afternoons

6 people wanted 'improved' chemists opening hours, and a more flexible rota whereby the duty chemist could fit in better with the closing times of doctors' surgeries

8 people wanted the Main Post Office open on Saturday afternoons, and earlier in the mornings

9 people wished that they could go back to having banks open on Saturday mornings.

29.6   When the girls had completed their survey and shown it to the Head, he thought it was so good that he sent a copy to the Town Clerk, who showed it to the Local Borough Council. Six-day shopping became the practice in the centre of town and the girls then went on to do further shopping surveys in the neighbourhood centres of Hemel Hempstead. Clearly, although making the survey involved them in necessary reading and writing skills, they were a long way from 'reading for reading's sake'. What they were finding out was how much the ordinary citizen can do to bring about change, and how little. They were proving the need to discover actual opinion before being able to translate it into effective action and they were finding out about the apathy of some of their elders. For fourth year students about to enter the adult world it was an excellent introduction to what they could expect to find. Like examples 16, 21, 22, 24, 26 and 28, it was taking the pupils out into the community they knew while offering relevance within the school curriculum.

30

A Bran-tub

30.1   In collecting materials for this monograph I have been offered several suggestions by teachers for activities which have not yet been carried out but might be in the future. There have also been accounts of activities which were not fully developed and of some which took place in the past and left no remaining examples of materials. Although perhaps none of these examples warranted a section to itself, rather than exclude good teaching ideas, I have grouped them together at the end. Their common basis is that they all await development and that they all offer reading, writing and relevance.

One suggestion for younger children, related to school tasks (see example 10), was that, as a variant on the list and rota principle, children whose turn it was to do something in class should pick cards from a group placed face downwards. What was written on the card would be instructions for a particular task, but it would be up to the teacher to vary the cards and their wording as much as possible, so that children were not just guessing the task by memorising non-linguistic features on the card.

Another suggestion was that, since children watch a lot of television and discuss what programmes they have seen and what they expect to see, the making of a classroom *TV Times* would be a relevant and useful project. Because the same programmes come round each week, the vocabulary is repeated and reinforced, together with the words for days of the week and so on. It is valuable exercise in planning and selection, as well as involving reading and writing. It also provides an opportunity to discuss programme preferences and the reasons for them and, over a period of time, leads to more thoughtful evaluation of TV programmes. This kind of evaluation can then be linked to the children's evaluation of the books they are reading.

Leaving notes between teacher and children was another idea. A teacher with responsibility for the library leaves notes for library monitors on their desks and often receives notes from them. Another one is in the habit of leaving a note attached to the place where apparatus is usually kept if it has been moved elsewhere for any reason.

Planning a holiday was a possible junior school activity. This suggestion arose from class discussion of where the children were going for their holidays. Noting possible resources for information about holiday areas, compilation of their own brochures for the area they were interested in before going there, or making such an information folder for storage on their return, are all reading and writing connected with this interesting but seasonal subject. Remember the teacher's warning in 16.2 before tackling such a project.

Two further activities connected with pets were suggested—what an important resource those guinea-pigs are! Finding out about animal growth, starting with the baby rabbits and gerbils in the classroom, is closely related to children's own lives. Measuring skills are exercised, not only as applied to the animal's height, length, weight, girth, and so on, but also in relation to food and water intake, and records and reports can be made, read and evaluated. The other suggestion is perhaps more appropriate for older juniors: finding out if pets can learn. Children often express interest in what animals can do and notice when they do something new. Simple conditioning experiments can be done with classroom pets, using food rewards and colours and symbols as stimuli. Again records of learning would be kept. When I read this suggestion, which certainly could be developed as a functional reading activity, I wondered if young junior school children would see just how relevant some aspects of it are to the way in which reading is often taught by stimulus/response/reward techniques! Perhaps the most valuable aspect of this activity would be for children to see how human and animal learning differs.

Weather forecasts were also suggested by a teacher in a rural/coastal area. Weather conditions were very important there for the fishing and farming which formed many of their parents' occupations and the children were very aware of them. Prediction on one day is checked the next and various ways of forecasting are discussed, from what happens at the Meteorological Office to folk beliefs about cows lying down and the use of seaweed. Records of predictions need to be kept in order for them to be checked against actual events so that children can begin to learn about probability. Communication between schools could be used for the collection and combination of data for greater reliability and information on local weather variations.

Instructions for using a telephone was another suggestion for young juniors, who were encouraged to ring home with messages like, 'Please could you bring my swimming things?', and to answer incoming 'phone-calls in the school. Another little girl was helped over her nervousness of telephones by looking up all the services she could ring (like recipes, weather reports, story-telling) and then ringing them!

In the course of a discussion with a group of teachers about what constituted a 'guinea-pig activity' and what didn't, an example was given of counting the cars that went past the gates of the school as an obviously pointless exercise. Another teacher in the group countered with, 'It all depends what you're doing it for. Suppose you're counting the traffic to see if it's sufficient to get a lollipop-lady for outside the school—it's not pointless then!' Exactly.

Part 4

Out of School

31
Adult Literacy and Relevance

31.1   A tutor of adult illiterates received a request for relevant reading activities from a thirty-four-year-old man. He was a barman by trade and found that, although he knew the names of all the drinks his customers asked for and could get some of them right by the shape of the bottle or colour of the liquid, in many cases he still needed to be able to read the words on the labels. Consider all the different brands of whisky in their similar bottles, which all have faithful adherents who would be annoyed at seeing the barman reach for X when they asked for Y. Of course the tutor responded to the adult's need and most adult literacy tutors are aware of the need for working from the reading and writing which their students encounter in their lives. Even if you have never taught an adult, a pause for thought about reading in everyday life will produce some such list as this:

– roadsigns for vehicles
– signs for pedestrians: 'Cross now', 'Danger—men at work', etc.
– other signs and notices, 'Push/Pull', 'In case of fire—break glass', 'No Smoking', 'Ladies', 'Private', 'Wet Paint', etc.
– instructions at a self-service petrol station
– bus and train time tables
– instructions for washing-machines and dryers at the laundrette
– menus and pricelists in cafés, restaurants, etc.
– instructions in 'phone booths

This is by no means exhaustive. Anyone teaching an adult illiterate would be far more likely to make a note of all the public reading material he or she encountered in the course of the week than to get out a reading scheme, even if there were one aimed at that age-group.

31.2   So in the teaching of adults, functional reading seems to have caught on as the best means of keeping the interest and motivation of the student engaged with the work. But the public reading environment is as much there for a child as it is for an adult. A selection of the encounters with print which every child is likely to have in the course of a week might remove some examples from the adult list but many would remain which are often never considered in the teaching of reading. If you do use a reading scheme, ask yourself, if the age of the characters were changed, would it satisfy the daily requirements of an adult beginning reader. If the answer is no, reconsider why it seems appropriate for the needs of a child beginning reader living in the same language-filled environment.

32

Relevance and Parents

32.1   This section is not about how parents can help children in pre- and extra-school situations to be aware of the use and value of language. Such a subject provides material for a book on its own. What follows is merely a handful of suggestions for parents to encourage functional reading in the home.

Cliff-hanging   Perhaps the oldest ploy in the world for getting young children who have the rudiments of reading to do some for themselves is in the bedtime story situation. The parent reads, from a book whose vocabulary and structure are within the child's capabilities, up to a very exciting point and then stops for that session, making sure the book is left behind. The 'what happens next?' motivation is one of the strongest there is for reading.

Notes   For slightly older children, when parents can't be at home on their return from school, a note is a useful source of information as well as a comforting sign of attention. Some parents gave me actual examples of notes commonly left for their children.

★ Dear Jill,
        Please leave the cat in the kitchen when you go out to play,   Mummy
Have gone to the shops, back soon.

★ Jim . . .

I wont be home till 6. Do your homework so you can watch TV *after dinner*.
        Love,
            Mummy

These are notes from parent to child, but they often come in the other direction too, from the simple,

★ Mum, have gone out, back 6 pm. Paul   (age 13)

to the sophisticated,

★ Woman harpist from Cambridge, odd name, 'phoned. Will ring back later.

If the parent responds in the appropriate way to such notes, awareness of the point of writing and reading is reinforced. Finally, under notes, come two which were read by people other than the intended recipients.

★ Dear teeth Angels I lost my tooth under the seat of my car please can you find for me and give me the money.   (age 6)

★ Dear Santa,
Thank you very much for bringing all those presents in the past years. I think you are very kind.
    for this Christmas would you be so kind as to get me 1 Lego S.7, one S.17 and supplementary pack No. 431. My very good wishes for a happy Christmas.
            Love
                Paul

P.S. The mince pie and the apple are for you and your reinder
            Love
                Paul   (age 8)

Both examples of writing proved highly functional as far as results were concerned!

Television As in the previous section (30.1), it has been suggested that television, far from replacing reading, can be the means of promoting it. At the most basic level, the choosing of programmes to watch should involve reading the details and planning. One parent of older children said, 'Mine usually read the preview criticisms on programmes', which is a more sophisticated approach to the medium. Whenever a book is adapted for television, its sales show a marked increase, so there is some argument for believing that the 'box' introduces more people to books and reading than it beguiles away from them.

Lists   A busy working parent told me that, to be sure that each child has the right kit for the right day at school, there is a list on the kitchen wall, which reads:

Monday	Liz	P.E.
		Drama
	Rod	P.E.
Tuesday	Liz	Games
		Art
	Nick	Swimming etc.

On another part of the kitchen wall is a list of menus for tea for the week so that the first person home can start to get the meal. These are both examples taken from homes of children in their early teens, but there is no reason why such functional writing and reading shouldn't be present in younger families. Who writes notes for the milkman in your family? Do these necessary chores need to be done by an adult?

33

Conclusion

33.1   In encouraging children to engage in the many kinds of reading and writing activity described in this monograph, teachers will be helping them to become increasingly self-reliant and responsible. This in itself may be ample justification but, as far as reading is concerned, it is a bonus. It is just such opportunities as these which give children the best chance of becoming voluntary readers for pleasure and information. So when you are choosing between activities of various possible kinds, it is worth asking, 'How much reading will this involve? And for how many?' If all teachers look at the curriculum from this standpoint, there is a chance of developing a higher level of literacy in the next generation of adults. Reading and writing without relevance can only be meaningless mysteries.

Index